A Visit to Haldeman and Other States of Mind

Charles L. Mee, Jr.

A Visit to Haldeman and Other States of Mind

M. EVANS AND COMPANY, INC. / NEW YORK, N.Y. 10017

M. Evans and Company titles are distributed in
the United States by the J. B. Lippincott Company,
East Washington Square, Philadelphia, Pa. 19105;
and in Canada by McClelland & Stewart Ltd.,
25 Hollinger Road, Toronto M4B 3G2, Ontario

LIBRARY OF CONGRESS CATALOGING IN PUBLICATION DATA

Mee, Charles L
    A visit to Haldeman and other states of mind.

    1. Mce, Charles L.   2. United States—Biography.
3. Watergate Affair, 1972-   I. Title.
CT275.M46554A38 1977 070.4'092'4 [B] 76-30775
ISBN 0-87131-229-8

Design by Joel Schick

Manufactured in the United States of America

9 8 7 6 5 4 3 2 1

The quotation from 'The New Narcissism" is re-
printed by permission of International Creative Management for Peter Marin, © 1975 by Peter Marin.

For my parents' grandchilden—
Bruce, Mark, Craig, Christopher, Elizabeth,
Sylvie and Julie,
and Erin and Charles

By its nature, this book is all acknowl-edgments, however incomplete, and I could not make up for its many omis-sions in a brief note; I wish to acknowledge, however, that I could not have remembered or made sense of my own past without the help of Terka Julay, and that the book itself was virtually drawn out of me by Herb Katz.

One

IN the spring of 1975 just before I left my place in Greenwich Village for a journey to Beverly Hills, I had a lunch date with Richard Cape at one o'clock on the Upper East Side at Nicola's. Richard was one of the people I liked to be around just then to shore up my cynicism in case I felt myself slipping. It was a brilliant, crisp, newly scrubbed day, and Richard was broke and resplendent, not having had taxi fare, having walked from the Fifth Avenue apartment where he had been visiting for the past few months; he was dressed in an impeccably tailored blue blazer, Oxford cloth shirt open at the neck, a silk neckerchief with minuscule, abstract red and white flowers on a blue ground, soft gray flannel slacks, argyle socks, and a pair of soft brown leather loafers that fit like gloves, evidently custom-made. His hair had been newly dyed, jet black with flecks of gray at the temples, and he looked like a million dollars before taxes.

Richard moves in the worlds of politics and finance, of embezzlement, larceny, and war, with uncommon ease, and he is a man of profound principles. I once told him that one of his business ideas was indecent, and he responded, "Listen, Charles"—everyone but Richard calls me Chuck—"Listen, Charles, it is uncalled for and untoward to charge me with indecency. I have known decency and indecency in my time. I have known virtue and villainy. I have walked in the valleys and on the hillsides of decency. I have walked in the sunshine and in the shadows of decency." (Here he chokes up.) "I have walked on the coastlines of decency and waded in the chill rivulets of decency. I have descended into the hoary pits of decency, and I have climbed the lofty, swooning stupas of decency. I have walked the long, clean corridors of decency and" —here he weeps and cries out—"and I have had decency by the short hairs! Do you hear me, Charles? By the short hairs in my time! Do you know what I mean? Hunh? D'yunnerstan'? By the short hairs! Don't talk to *me* about decency."

Nothing embarrasses Richard. Nothing offends him. Nothing seems inconceivable to him. Nothing strikes him as either too wonderful to be true or too horrible to be a proposition worth entertaining. Nothing frightens him.

Richard was born fifty-odd years ago in Chicago. He has spent his life, for the most part, dodging in and out of politics, working a time for Adlai Stevenson in the Presidential campaigns of 1952 and 1956 and then, when John Kennedy ran for President, raising money and doing political polling for the Kennedy organization. He put all of his polling material on computer tapes, and, whacking around with random inputs and dazzling outputs and abstruse analyses by professors of political science, he claimed to have predicted John Kennedy's victory in 1960 within one tenth of 1 percentage point three months before the election occurred. He parlayed this stunning prediction into a corporate think tank. He put his corporation at the service of the State Department and the Defense Department—and the Defense Department apparently put him to work in Vietnam.

I first met him when his company had something to do with the planning of the pacification program in Vietnam, and I endeared myself to him then by telling him that I thought the war was both unwinnable and morally reprehensible. I thought at the time that he must be up to his armpits in war crimes, and I have never learned since precisely what it was his company did in Vietnam. But I got to know him as a man who

5

moves among politicians, political hacks and gofers, spies and counterspies, Pentagon generals and political rip-off artists.

In the course of a conversation we once had about going into business together, after his think tank went bankrupt following the Tet offensive in Vietnam, he introduced me to a fellow named Teddy who told me of a business he, Teddy, had once started in Rome. He realized that Americans have an inordinate fear of getting diarrhea while they're traveling abroad in Europe, and that they attribute this diarrhea not to the vast numbers of gallons of wine that they choke down in their European spree but to the water that they drink. It occurred to Teddy that he could make a fortune by selling American bottled water to American tourists. He raised five thousand dollars for his business scheme, and he went out with the five thousand dollars and bought as many old bottles as he could and went to a printing shop and got a printer to make some labels shaped like huge golden American eagles, on which was printed the legend: *American Bottled Water*. Having spent his five thousand dollars, he then took his bottles down to a Roman fountain, filled the bottles with water, stuck his labels on them, and sold the stuff as American bottled water to American tourists. This is the kind of businessman Richard Cape knew, and so I thought it was important for me to stay in touch with him.

I suppose that Richard, with his support of the Vietnam War and other murky diversions, did as much as

anyone to lay waste to the American Republic, and—
though I kept this knowledge from myself for most of
the years I knew him—it was doubtless for that reason
that I liked hanging around with him. He was my rotten self, and I sinned through him vicariously, skirting
and sometimes plunging into disaster. He seemed always, by dint of his corruption, to have some special
knowledge or strength that would redeem him—a
knowledge that, if it was not mysteriously special,
might simply be the knowledge of the eternal weakness
of human nature, and the names of his fellow humans
who had shared in his weakness and were thus bound
to him.

Once in Puerto Rico, the only time I've been there,
Richard and his friend Simonetta, and my wife, Suzi,
and I stayed in the condominium of one of Richard's
political acquaintances. (To whom do I owe a favor
now—the Milk Fund, an oil company, the CIA?) We
spent the days on the beaches talking good, decent, generous liberal politics, and swimming, and having lunch
and drinking, and we spent the evenings in casinos. One
evening, after a longish day in which Richard and I
had drunk a good deal while discussing whether draft
dodgers and war protesters should be exiled to Eugene
McCarthy's hometown in Minnesota, we fetched up at
one of the more stylish casinos, and, as the bouncer at
the door noticed, Richard had neglected to wear socks.
House rule: no sockless patrons in the casino. Perhaps
they did not know who Richard was? It did not matter;
the house rule was inflexible. How could the house rule

be inflexible? Did this fellow—what was his name and position incidentally?—did this fellow not unnerstan' that some rules were meant to be bent when certain . . . ah . . . people presented themselves at the door? Where was the manager? Busy. Ah-ha. In that case (Richard turned to Simonetta), would Simonetta step into the ladies' room for a moment?

Richard and Simonetta (Once, when she was gone for a long time in San Juan with Suzi, and I was worried, Richard said: "Ah, fuck, you don't have to worry about her; she's CIA, ya know. She'd kill anyone gave her trouble; ya know what I mean? She doesn't give a shit, she'd as soon kill someone as anything; as a matter of fact, I think she'd *like* to kill someone in San Juan; she's a mean son of a bitch") stepped off to the side of the lobby, and Richard whispered to the lovely, gentle Simonetta, who loved Richard and would do anything he said, and then she disappeared into the ladies' room, emerged a few minutes later, handed something to Richard, who disappeared into the men's room and then reappeared at the door to the casino—wearing Simonetta's pantyhose for socks.

Ah, well, to be sure, sir, there could be no question that he was properly attired as regards his ankles—of course, to be sure, pantyhose were unquestionably acceptable, sir—but he was not wearing a tie!

Richard asked Suzi to step into the ladies' room. Suzi disappeared, emerged, Richard disappeared, emerged, stepped up to the door to the casino—wearing Suzi's pantyhose around his neck.

8

Unacceptable? Who the fuck do you think you are, you? . . . and so forth.

The four of us appeared in the manager's office within a few minutes. The manager, seated coolly, calmly behind his desk, with a cigarette in a silver cigarette holder, spoke quietly and pleasantly, in a melodious and rich voice, well-modulated and welcoming. He was surrounded by four large guys standing.

Richard said he would like a Chivas Regal on the rocks.

The manager nodded. One of the goons went to fetch the drink.

Cigarette?

Richard took the manager's offer of a cigarette.

This is, Richard said casually, condescendingly, encouragingly to the manager as he took a cigarette, a lovely casino; he remembered it fondly; but was it not under new management since the last time he had been here?

When was that?

Oh, that would have been a couple of years before when he came with A., the prime minister.

(I can remember none of the names Richard tossed into the conversation, they came too quickly and trippingly from his tongue.)

Indeed?

Yes, it would have been with A. and with B., his deputy. Did the manager by any chance know B?

Yes, in fact, the manager did know B.

Ah, what a coincidence! Alas, Richard had not had

a chance to call B. this time in Puerto Rico. How was he?

Why did they not find out? said the manager. Would Richard like to talk to B.? The manager would get him on the phone.

Wonderful!

A goon dialed at a phone in one corner.

Incidentally, Richard inquired, had the manager sen C. or D. around the casino recently?

No, C. was not in Puerto Rico that month.

Ah, what a shame. Richard had especially enjoyed C.'s wife, E., and his brother-in-law, G., and the brother-in-law's friend M. How was M.?

The manager did not know M.

The goon put down the phone and said there was no answer.

RICHARD: Did the manager by any chance want to try to call X., Y., or Z., in that case, just to say hello for old times' sake? Or perhaps—and here Richard laughed —the local chief of police, S.

Well . . .

Richard was running at full tilt now: Perhaps the manager would like to call the prime minister's personal secretary, R., or the secretary's wife, L., or the sheriff's brother-in-law's best friend, H.

No, no, no, not just then, the lateness of the hour, the press of business. Would Richard like another drink? No, thank you, Richard would not care for another drink. The night was young, and Richard wanted to show his friends some of Puerto Rico's night life. He would not embarrass the manager by insisting upon going back to the casino downstairs; we would move along to another spot; it had been a pleasure chatting; please give his best regards to B.

Would Richard and his friends care to have the manager's car to take them on to another casino?

How very kind of the manager, but no, thank you, our car would be waiting for us.

In that case . . .

Once again . . .

Not at all . . .

And so Richard and Simonetta and Suzi and I walked out the front door of that place with Richard still swathed in pantyhose. There was no car waiting for us. The exit was anticlimactic, I thought. I told Richard that the manager would be looking out the window and see that we had no car and have his suspicions aroused.

"Aw, fuck 'em. He knew I was bullshitting him all along."

I always thought I should try to reform Richard, especially that I should try to get him to change his mind about the Vietnam War. By not arguing against him forcibly enough to get him to turn around, I was, as they say, sharing in his guilt. But I did not want to reform Richard, any more than he wanted to corrupt me; that would have spoiled it. We needed each other; we amused each other; we kept each other alive—just as villainy and naïveté, supporting one another, have kept America alive in my lifetime.

In any case, since we were there having lunch together, and Richard knew the sorts of things he knows, and then, too, in order to pass the time of day, I thought I might ask Richard's advice about my imminent departure for Beverly Hills. I had been asked several days before whether or not I would care to collaborate on a book with H. R. Haldeman; and I was on my way to California to meet with the old malefactor.

Haldeman no longer has the fierce hold he once had on our imaginations. Now the precise Teutonic disciplinarian, the crew-cut administrator, harsh and cruel, has mellowed in our vague memories; now, in retrospect, he seems merely smooth and insincere; but, back when he was the right-hand man to Richard Nixon, and later, after Haldeman resigned amid the holy clamor for the removal of his boss, he had seemed formidable enough.

The book deal with which I had been presented was that I talk to Haldeman, write something that gave his point of view fairly, and then feel perfectly free to write whatever I wished as commentary. I was to be a kind of coauthor, a critical annotator in the making of an historical record—a collaborator.

As I went on talking about the deal, Richard commenced to look increasingly uneasy, to glance around the restaurant restlessly, and to make distracting little motions and noises with his package of Pall Mall cigarettes, as though he were trying to mess up the functioning of the tape recorder hidden under the table.

He made me exceedingly nervous, this man whom nothing fazed. Finally, after I had finished, Cape looked around the restaurant, leaned close over the table, lowered his voice, and spoke.

CAPE: Don't do it. That's all. That's all I'm saying. Don't be an asshole.

His fear was infectious. What did he mean? He would not explain. But, then, I did not need his explanation. He knew that there was no way I could escape from Haldeman with my honesty intact. It might even have been, so Richard seemed to imply, that Haldeman still had some connections with Washington people, with certain kinds of people, with certain . . . ah . . . agents, for instance, who had, well, ways, certain ways of doing things and, ah, persuading people to do certain things. At the very least, if one was not to be unduly anxious about it, Haldeman was assuredly a clever manipulator, far cleverer than I; that was, after all, why he had been where he had been. I would be used. Somehow. There could be no doubt of that.

In fact, was it not true that I had already imagined myself, in one of my unacknowledged fantasies, hero of liberalism, championing Haldeman's despised cause? Had it not already occurred to me that, in fact, Haldeman might actually turn out to be innocent and that I, good, courageous, liberal-minded seeker of truth, might be the one to cast aside my old prejudices, throw off the blinders, look anew at his case and see, finally, that Haldeman was innocent! God! how I would then tell his story: so eloquently, with such conviction, so thrillingly, with such a deep and soaring ring of authenticity. I, single-handedly, would root out the unpopular truth and have the selfless bravery to tell it, enduring the scorn of friends and the unjust obloquy of strangers.

I was a pushover. I actually wanted to be seduced by the guy.

And then I was struck with a sudden terror. Wanting as I did to be seduced by this surrogate-father-brother, man of staunchness and of the secrets of power and corruption, I was abruptly riven by the fear that I might in fact be debauched by him, and forced, coerced, induced into performing bizarre, distasteful acts. And, as if that were not enough, perhaps after Haldeman had used me according to his will, he would then have me bundled off in the back seat of a limousine to—where? To what end? To have me killed for refusing to cooperate with his designs for rehabilitating his reputation? To have me brainwashed perhaps. Perhaps to strap the steel cap to my head, pierce my skull with the electrodes, frazzle my brain, and then commence the long, slow process of dripping and oozing into my consciousness only those facts and interpretations and feelings he wanted there.

Or perhaps not. Perhaps we were headed instead for San Clemente where we would meet the Dark Liar himself, and he, it would turn out, he, the Dark Liar, would have my dossier.

"It's a pleasure to see you, Mr. Mee," the Liar

would say, sliding a fat folder from one side of the polished desk to the other, tapping it absently with his wrinkled fingers. "I know you're going to want to be fair in anything you write. I certainly hope, after you've had a chance to spend some time with Bob, that you'll at least understand our point of view, maybe even sympathize with it." A smile here. "Who knows?"

He would not have to say any more. They would all know what was in that dossier. Anyway, the Liar would know, and I would suspect. Had they found out about the masturbation?

Such dreams as these, vague and confused with homosexual fantasies, are kid stuff these days. If only our dreams were entirely sexual, however deviant, we might feel relieved. But there are more rampant, flamboyant fantasies in our age of common, epidemic impotence—a symptom, if yet one more is needed, of the shambles of our shared, public world—and those are the fantasies of power.

The history of power politics, as the English historian and philosopher Karl Popper has written with exemplary detachment and cool, "is nothing but the history of international crime and mass murder (including, it is true, some of the attempts to suppress them). This history is taught in schools, and some of the greatest criminals are extolled as its heroes." Why, Popper puts the rhetorical question, is not the history of mankind written as the history of religion or poetry? "There are several reasons. One is that power affects us all, and poetry only a few. Another is that men are inclined to worship power. But there can be no doubt that the worship of power is one of the worst kinds of human idolatries, a relic of the time of the cage, of human servitude, the worship of power is born of fear, an emotion which is rightly despised."

Moved by this despicable emotion, we of the twentieth century—or I at least—dream no longer only or simply of sex, but also of power, or of sex and power. That sex and power are so intermingled in our dreams is—no doubt of it—partly explained by our own psychologies alone; but it is only completely explained by seeing ourselves, political animals all, as members of a community, too, as citizens, too, in a shattered Republic, dismayed by our impotence in the larger community, frightened and disoriented by our powerlessness in the public arena, fearing and lusting for power, wishing to seduce, or to be seduced and protected, living in an anguish of real and imagined chaos and brutality.

This is the curse of our century: to be ravaged by power run mad, unchecked, and nightmarish—power in all its forms, from gentle, Skinnerian persuasion and manipulation to grotesqueries of violence, from the neutralization of our individual wills to the cool use of our bodies, from the unfelt but sometimes suspected suasions to the unwilling deliverance of our flesh to gas and bombs and flames. This is, in any case, my own curse, to live in fascination and fear of power, and I know my nightmare is shared by some at least: I see them, sleepwalkers, in the streets, and some of them carry guns.

The problem, as I told myself that afternoon after lunch, walking out of Nicola's restaurant, strolling down past the tobacconists and news dealers of Lexington Avenue, is that the Republic is dead. I had not wished to admit the fact, but there it was, and I no longer had the strength or wish to hold it off, resisting it, saying maybe not, it is not dead, or perhaps it is not so, qualifying here and there, tucking it in at the edges, neatening it up, smoothing over, hoping no one will notice, fearful of finding myself mad or radical or, in giving up the ghost of hope, encouraging the end, bringing on tyranny, ringing up the curtain, striking up the band of jackbooted agents of the police state, giving birth to a new holocaust by whispering of the death of the dear departed Republic. And yet it is dead. Its death is palpable.

All is symptomatic; all are the predicted events that follow the collapse of a Republic—the citizens who do not vote, the businessmen whose corrupted and corrupting loyalties transcend the borders of their native land, the presidents and others who lurk about hiding their acts from the people and employing sneaks to spy upon their own fellow citizens, public servants who presume to play at being masters, the foreign policy makers who try to distract our gaze by crying wolf here and there as the wily monarchs of old once did, arousing us to this or that external threat while all the time, the death comes from within: yes they, too; and even now, in the heat of our argument, do trivial food fads seem symptoms of hedonism gone awry, of individualism run amok, of private Epicurean self-seeking gone mad in a rush of deficit spending, cutting back, Scientology, growth centers, turning away from the shared public world to privatism and Erhard Seminar Training. The ruins of our Republic lie about us, like shards of some other ancient dead civilization.

And that is O.K. In fact, it's about time. Its death was overdue, and the family stood about for quite some time shifting from one foot to the other, glancing at wristwatches, wondering when deliverance would come, knowing we had other things to do, a life to get on with, and the predictions of death, the last ministrations, the laments, the breast-beatings, and regrets, the last gasping fears or hopes, that the prognosis might change at the end and that the patient might revive, and all the rest of it were getting to be—and let us acknowledge it forthrightly—altogether tiresome. It had become a nuisance to have the decrepit Republic hanging around making demands on our emotions and loyalties so long after it was obviously time for it to kick off. And so, finally, it did. *Requiescat. Pax.*

Yes, to be sure, the Republic will be reborn, or reincarnated in a somewhat new guise—for the republican form of government is a remarkably hardy form, a perennial, easy to stamp out or dig out or burn off from time to time, but hard to get rid of permanently.

It *will* pop up again. But I hasten on too quickly, averting my eyes from the corpse.

Dare we admit that we did not at first notice? That it died when no one was looking, and we scarcely missed it for days or, it may even be, for years? We only first noticed it, reluctantly, wishing not to see, when Nixon buggered the works, and then buggered those who went after him, a Bulgar holding out against the hordes until at last, unimpeachable, he was told he must step down—not by Congress and not by the courts but by four-star General Haig in a pinch play with Bad Kissinger, and then—oh, God, where is our sense of shame?—pardoned by his handpicked successor for crimes he protested he did not commit. We said it proved the Republic worked, but we knew that Republics are not saved when their constitutional usages are forgotten or avoided and salvation depends upon the accidents of a tape recording machine and the wits of a four-star general. Machiavelli could not do justice to this theme. Shakespeare's Richard II could not weep copiously enough. We watched it play itself out, with the nerves of dead men in a dead Republic.

And then we found that the Republic had not died with Richard Nixon—but had, in truth, died long before, when no one was looking and no one noticed, and now no one could even remember when it had been. Rigor mortis had already passed, long since; the muscles were relaxed once again, the ashen face looked calm enough, and peaceful, content even and contented, pleasant and easygoing, in short a friendly and familiar corpse of whom we had all grown fond without quite knowing why. We had, indeed, grown accustomed to it; we were comfortable with it; we did not want it moved out, or touched, or altered.

It is dead. That is not to say that the brownshirted totalitarians have taken over. No, not yet. Now a more or less benevolent more or less oligarchy more or less rules. Some are pleased by this. Some say it has always been so. Some say it is not true—and continue to praise the oligarchy, thinking it is still a Republic, thankful when order has been more or less restored, thinking the Republic has been restored when it is only that the oligarchs have got things stuck together again. And so we applaud and cheer—no longer acting citizens in a Republic but fans at a baseball game—praising this one, voting for that one, rooting for the other one, happy with the noise and the color of the distant spectacle.

When did this unfortunate state devolve? Certainly it seemed worth knowing. It appeared that the Republic had once been alive and well—not perfect to be sure, never ideal of course—but alive and well and capable of growth and improvement. Alexis de Tocqueville, touring America in 1831, had reported on a country that still had slavery and some other, lesser evils, some dislocations of wealth and power and privilege, some total exclusion of women from the polity, but a Republic nonetheless, one worth preserving and extending, enriching and deepening. And then, sometime between the time of Tocqueville and our own time, it ceased to grow; it stopped; its sinews atrophied, its juices dried, it ossified in the form of oligarchy, and died. Sometime, it seemed, or so the common wisdom went, after the robber barons, after Tammany Hall, after the Spanish-American War and World War I and the twenties, even after the Great Depression, after Roosevelt, sometime, finally, in fact, within my own lifetime. But when? I thought I might get some clue from Haldeman—if I could look at him clearly, without blinking.

Certainly there, in any event, standing there on Lexington Avenue, lost in thought, staring fixedly into the shop window of Mini-Mundus, with its tidy little displays of antique doll-house furniture, its little nineteenth-century parlors, tea trays, candelabra, doilies, its tiny quilts and tatting and pewter plates—standing, staring, and, it may even be, muttering—was not going to help.

That afternoon, after lunch with Richard, I had an appointment to stop by for a moment to transact a small bit of business at the offices of David Susskind over on Third Avenue. Susskind had bought the rights to my history of the Potsdam Conference, and I had been given some contracts to look over and sign and then return to his offices. When I took the contracts up to the offices, which looked like one of Woody Allen's visions of a television producer's office in the year 3000,

Susskind came out to say hello to me. Susskind is a little guy. In fact, he is almost tiny. Indeed, you could almost put Susskind in your lunchbox.

He is also covered with makeup. I don't understand why Susskind should be covered with makeup at three o'clock in the afternoon, but there he was, covered with makeup about four or five inches thick, about as thick as he is tall. I liked him. He has extraordinary energy. He came out of his office like a high-tension transmission wire that had been cut and sprung loose, pure, flowing, slashing energy. It is remarkable to see so much energy coming from such a little guy, who looks like a very small Emmy Award. He asked me what I was up to and I told him.

SUSSKIND: You do that? You do that???? Listen [face red, finger jabbing], I saw that rotten bastard son of a bitch at a meeting of the Young Presidents in Aspen, and I said to him, "Listen, you goddamned son of a bitch, how do you like being responsible for destroying the faith of a whole generation, a whole generation!, of young people in their country! goddamn it!" That son of a bitch! goddamn it! [retreating to his office, withdrawing from me, the collaborator, as though from a leper, face red, finger jabbing] that son of a bitch! goddamn it!

I was left, abandoned, alone, in the cavernous, year-3000 reception area of Susskind's offices. A secretary, mute and stony, was immobile to my left, staring at me. The receptionist, seated behind her commodious plastic *escritoire* could not meet my gaze:

she looked down at the empty, glistening top of her desk, reading it. I had to wait for the elevator, pinned there, unable either to look at my accusers or turn my back on them.

It had occurred to me by this time that I was not prepared to meet H. R. Haldeman. I was not prepared in spirit, in background briefings or inquisitorial training; I had no idea what I was doing. Nor did I have time to repair my ignorance or my psychological faults or my interrogatory technique; but I could at least ask someone else what questions to ask Haldeman to induce him to reveal what he knew. At the very least I ought to be equipped with those inquiries that would so assault Haldeman as to cause him to exhale sharply, hissing through his teeth, crumple to the ground, and tell all, beginning with his primal experiences.

I went to see Charles Morgan, who was the head of the Washington office of the American Civil Liberties Union, and who had been the national director of the ACLU impeachment campaign. He would be, I thought, a man who had had reason to keep in touch with theories about the meaning of the ungracious departure of Nixon and Haldeman and the others from Washington, and I flew to Washington to see him. I knew Morgan. I did not know him well, but we had spoken to one another from time to time during Nixon's last days in the White House.

I first met Morgan when I was a founder and the chairman of the National Committee on the Presidency, a nationwide, grass-roots, citizens' organization

CHARLES L. MEE, JR.

of some thousands of good middle-of-the-road, respectable decent people very like you and me from all the great fifty states who desired and lobbied tirelessly and selflessly for the constitutional removal of the President from his office for the sake of the Republic and the preservation of American liberty in the face of threatened tyranny; and somehow, for some reason, though we raised many generous small contributions and enlisted thousands of followers and mailed hundreds of thousands of letters and my friend and co-founder Ted Zimmermann, a large, teddy-bear-shaped, mustachioed and breathtakingly honest lawyer from the Middle West, and I tramped the halls of Congress on behalf of this good cause, it all turned to disappointment and absurdity and despair over the working of constitutional government as an expression of the manifest will of the people when Nixon resigned and ducked down the back stairs—a sensation that I was trying to explain to a straightforward tough-minded Chicagoan one evening in a New York bar, when he said, swigging a beer and smacking his lips, "Yeah, it was a real jerk-off."

Morgan is a man who had been on the front lines of the civil rights marches in the late fifties and into the sixties, a man who had been hanging around Capitol Hill, knew what a congressman was, and knew what Washington was. His office was on the Hill, back behind the Capitol building, on the shabby side of Washington, at the edge of a bleak, but respectable and upwardly mobile, black slum.

24

He is a large, fattening, pasty-complexioned, southern drawler, straight-talker, sheriff-type feller, who only needs galluses and a cigar and an old beat-up Model T to complete the picture of the corrupt southern pol, standing around the courthouse steps, spitting, swearing, knowing the deals, the fixes, which assemblyman has a shoebox full of bribe money, which one got the road contract from whose nephew. Morgan emerged from his office, a hulking shambles of a man, bearing down on his visitor like a giant amoeba with mismatched socks: "Goddamn! Good to see you. How are you? Son of a bitch. Goddamn!"

I could not tell Morgan how I was. Morgan talks fast, and I could not get a word in edgewise. He closed on me and absorbed me into his office. Nor did I have a chance, once in his office, flung toward the couch like an attaché case full of legal briefs and used shirts, to ask Morgan any preliminary questions such as (a) tell me, Mr. Morgan, who killed the Republic, (b) when did this unhappy event occur, (c) what . . . He was already talking, building a case bit by bit—no matter whether his case was the one in which I happened to be interested—pulling it together, tossing out leads and drawing in inferences, arguing and hectoring his case together, and, as he went, causing me also to remember things unbidden.

MORGAN: OK, here's what to ask the bastard. Ask him to explain the relationship between Howard Hughes and the CIA. What, if any, effect did those relationships have on the Watergate case and other activities of the plumbers? What were the plumbers' other activities?

MEE: Are you . . .

MORGAN: I'll get to that later. What discussion occurred at the White House regarding the Hughes-Mayhew lawsuit? What relationship did Haig and Kissinger have with the CIA? When did it begin? Do you want a cup of coffee?

I was trying to write all this stuff down on the back of an old envelope. He was at his desk, sitting in a large swivel chair, his feet up, resting in a pile of papers. I was holding off a collapsing stack of briefs and petitions on one end of the couch and a pile of other papers and files on the other end, and with my third hand I was trying to make notes on Morgan's briefing—and I must have the report of our conversation nearly all wrong. I got to this last question about a cup of coffee and realized that Morgan wanted an answer from me.

MEE: Black.

MORGAN: [shouting] Could we have two black coffees?

The question was directed to the walls and ceiling. Presumably someone within a few blocks of the ACLU office would hear this question and respond. Meantime, I pressed on with my unfinished interrogatory.

MEE: Are you . . .

MORGAN: OK, list the types of activities in which CIA, naval intelligence, or like agencies are participating in the ocean.

MEE: You mean the story about the *Glomar Explorer:* Hughes's ship, about bringing up the Russian sub . . .

MORGAN: May be a cover. What is everyone doing down in the oceans? What's down there? While everyone has been looking at the moon for the past fifteen years, what has the government been doing underwater? Are there missiles down there? Maybe Nixon told the truth when he said Watergate compromised the national security. Why was Watergate bugged? Why bug Larry O'Brien? Well, Larry O'Brien worked for Howard Hughes, got paid fifteen thousand dollars a month. A month. Oliver—he's the guy whose phone was bugged at Democratic National Headquarters, remember, the bug on his phone worked—Oliver's father was a Hughes lobbyist. There are other connections: Howard Hunt's lawyer was Bittman; Bittman was a member of Hughes's law firm. Hunt worked for the Mullen firm, which was wholly owned by the CIA. Bennett, who also worked for Mullen, was a Woodward source. Who was Deep Throat? Was Deep Throat from the CIA? For that matter, how was Jaworski selected to be special prosecutor? Jaworski once paid money into a CIA front.

MEE: Are you telling me . . .

MORGAN: I'm not telling you anything. I'm asking questions. Thanks. You remember Chuck Mee?

Mrs. Morgan, smart, attractive, wearing sneakers, had materialized with coffee. Just as Morgan is large and hulking and booming, Mrs. Morgan is diminutive and quick and chirpy. She has also, as far as I can tell, been completely absorbed by Morgan, too.

Mrs. Morgan, anyhow, seems to be completely dedicated to bringing coffee to her husband. She may even be dedicated to her husband. In fact, it is possible—and the more I think about it, it seems likely—that Mrs. Morgan is even dedicated to the same principles that her husband embraces. So there are the two of them: embracing the same principles, embracing each other, and shoving piles of legal briefs off the couch onto the floor.

I don't know how many children the Morgans have, but while I was there that day, Morgan made some phone calls about a college-age son, who was intent upon getting into the same sort of public-interest racket that his father is in. The son wanted to get a job in investigative journalism, and it pleased me to see his father pulling strings, twisting arms, using his influence and contacts, wheedling and cajoling, as though he were a ward-heeling politician trying to get a post-office job for his nephew. From what I saw of it, the whole Morgan family is monomaniacal and, to me, completely congenial.

This sense of close, mutually supportive family strikes me with particular poignance. I have twice married, twice split up my marriages, and I miss my second wife if not my first. I miss that sense of extended family, the great manse filled with children and aunts and uncles and grandparents for which all human beings seem to long, all human beings seem to believe once existed in a previous century, and which the demographers tell us never did. Still, we long for it. It does represent an ideal human community. I am separated, and free, and enjoying my freedom; I would not dream of recommending to anyone else in the world that they stay in unhappy marriages; and yet, I do not think that all of the broken marriages point toward some ideal existence. The ideal is the great extended family—however rarely anyone ever achieves it.

I was first married when I was a student at Harvard. In those ancient days—I graduated in the class of 1960—I was doing a great deal of acting, writing for the theater, and directing. In celebration of the fiftieth anniversary of the Harvard Dramatic Club, I chose to direct Bertolt Brecht's *The Good Woman of Setzuan*—God alone knows why. Although in those days, plenty of young people proclaimed themselves Communists, at least for a time, I could never quite bring myself to declare myself a Communist. I hadn't the time. I was already too many other things: a deist, an artist, an ex-Catholic, and a few other roles that kept me fairly busy. What I liked about Brecht was simply that he was an aesthetic rebel. I once directed a Brecht play in a workshop production, in which I left on all the lights in the audience—and turned off all the stage lights.

As the Good Woman, I cast an extraordinarily beautiful young woman, with very large brown eyes and a truly magnificent look of total dependence. I

CHARLES L. MEE, JR.

now know that one should beware this look of dependence, as she doubtless knows one should beware anyone who accepts such a look of dependence, but we were both young then, and she needed someone to take care of her, and I needed to take care of someone. Neither of us got what we wanted.

We carried on a tortured, guilt-ridden, postadolescent love affair all that winter in Cambridge. I wish to God someone had got to us and told us just how two young people might be with each other in such a way as to get some shred of happiness. In those bad old days, a nice girl never had a love affair unless she married immediately thereafter. And so, though I think neither of us wanted it, and though we both gave each other a great deal of unhappiness, we were married the following summer at Stratford, Connecticut, where she was acting in the Shakespeare Festival.

The wedding was idyllic and youthfully romantic, out in the green grass surrounded by flowers and by the young players. It was a Hippie wedding years before there were Hippies. We were married between a matinee and an evening performance, as I recall, and for two young people who were smitten with the theater, nothing at all could have been more perfect than that.

Nothing was ever again quite as perfect as that. There were times of great pleasure. I remember one time in the autumn we went up to Nantucket, where her family had a summer home, and we wandered around the island, back among the dunes. We found there the stump of an old tree that had been burned in a fire on the island, and I dug up that weathered stump, working for days with an ax and saw and shovel and finally got the thing out of the ground. We took it back to her family's home and cleaned it up and finally made quite a handsome coffee table of the thing. We picked bayberries. We picked tons of bayberries. We picked bayberries for days and days. We had it in mind that we should make bayberry candles, and, though neither of us knew how to make bayberry candles, we went at it with the intensity and love and abandon of five-year-old children. We thought that what we had to do was boil these bayberries in a great pot of water so that the wax coating would come off the berries and float to the surface of the water, from which we would then skim it. Our plan was to transfer this wax, then, to another container, melt it down, and put wicks in it.

We got a huge old iron pot, filled it halfway with water, and set it in the middle of a great open fireplace in the living room. We lit a vast fire. We lit a tremendous fire. It blazed and roared. We threw on more and more wood. The fire burned all day. The water would not boil. We threw on more wood and more wood and the fire burned into the late afternoon. That miraculous Nantucket sunset finally competed with the fire in the spectacle of reds, yellows, and purples and oranges, until the sun went down, and we were left late into the night sitting in front of the fire. At last, in the middle of the night, the water commenced to bubble, and we threw in the bayberries and put more wood on the fire, and then spread pillows in front of the fireplace and lay down on the pillows and made love through the night in front of the fire. We must have been really extraordinarily beautiful. We were both so young, in our early twenties, and our bodies must have looked good together with the light of the fire playing across them through the night. We could be gentle and loving with one another. We could hold one another. We could brush a strand of hair back from one another's forehead, kiss each other's eyes, hold one another's head lightly but firmly, and drift with one another through space, through the night. But we were too young, and too confused, and too guilt-ridden, and too ignorant to deal with the passions we aroused in one another. As time went on, it seemed to me that principally what she wanted from me was to have me hurt her. I, a boy so eager to please, couldn't understand what kept me from pleasing her, or what motivated me sometimes when I did.

But it is Suzi, my second wife, who I really miss. She is the mother of my thirteen-year-old daughter and my seven-year-old son and it is with Suzi that I shared so many of my growing-up years, all through the sixties and into the seventies. It is the fashion now to despise the sixties, but I loved the sixties. I thought the sixties were what life was.

The sixties were hardly without an undertone of dark and fearful events. I came straight to New York from Harvard when I graduated, and was motivated finally to break up my first marriage by the Cuban missile crisis. On the night that John Kennedy went on television to announce that he might be having to push the button because the Russians were setting up missiles in Cuba, I went to the theater, to see an English troupe perform a series of satirical skits. Everyone in the theater knew, of course, of the presumed threat of sudden death. The English performers, however, had not thought to reconsider the material for their show in the light of the evening's news. At one point, they got into a skit about some sort of political tumult; the routine worked itself up into a climax of sorts, up to a punch line about—The Bomb. The audience gasped. I have never before nor since heard such a thing in a theater: As one, the whole audience gasped. And the performers did not regain the emotional following of that audience again until after the intermission. All of us had shared the identical thought, I believe—a thought that was absolutely new and very startling for an American. We realized that, for the first time in our experience, our very lives were in the hands of the President of our country. It was an extraordinary revelation. For the first time in the history of America, the President had somehow come to possess so much power as to make you gasp. And make me leave my wife—or provide, at least, a suitably melodramatic gloss. If I was to die, I told myself, I did not wish to die with my first wife—and so I left.

The sixties had a nuthouse streak that ran right through the decade. At the time of the missile crisis, my sometime friend André Gregory, an actor and director, lean and quick in his movements, with lank black hair that slashed across his left eye and across his face, giving him the energetic look of a Rasputin who took vitamin B_{12}, the young man who produced Jean Genet's *The Blacks* off-Broadway and, as I better knew, performed in a one-act play of mine in a crummy theater on East Ninth Street off Second Avenue, was rich. And then André heard that the missiles might go off at any time, he started buying airline tickets for all hours of the day and night for himself, his wife, and his child. He was ready to go at any moment, whether from rehearsal or from home, from the theater or from Sardi's, André was ready to go, and for several days when André would be sitting with me or some other friend in a dark, wet, rotting bar in Greenwich Village, he would excuse himself every half hour or so to go to the phone and—as he explained—cancel another reservation. He canceled perhaps half of his reservations and so only got stuck paying for half. All of André's airline flights were booked for Rio de Janeiro, which, André explained at length and in learned detail, was the one best place in the entire world, in case of nuclear war between America and Russia, to escape the fallout. It was some years later that I was idly studying a chart of nuclear fallout and noticed that, in the event of nuclear war in which missiles fell on Cuba, Rio de Janeiro was one

34

of the worst places in the universe to be. In the sixties, none of us had yet learned that politics is inescapable.

I was, of course, in my twenties then, and it was the first taste I had ever had in my life of independence, of being utterly on my own and making my own way. It never occurred to me in the 1960s that this was not the way life was going to be forever.

We had a wonderful time. Suzi was an actress, and I wrote plays for her, and we would hang around with friends of hers from Strasberg's Actors' Studio, and we went to the theater all the time. I had taken a job at American Heritage Publishing Company, and I was editing history books, but I was also, from time to time, taking a leave of absence, or quitting and coming back. I was an associate editor of the *Tulane Drama Review* and the editor of *Playbill* magazine, the theater program. So we always had theater tickets. We went to everything. We saw everything. We despised much. We loved a lot. We spent time backstage. We spent time at Sardi's and Downey's. We had tea in the Palm Court at the Plaza Hotel and drinks in the Oak Room and lunch at the Hotel New Weston. We had dinner at P.J. Clarke's, and we used to play chess and checkers and Go at Elaine's before Elaine's became one of the fashionable spots of the New York literati. I wonder where all of our money came from. God, we had a wonderful time. We saved not a penny. We spent all we had. We took taxis everywhere.

We lived in an apartment house on Tenth Street in Greenwich Village between Fifth and Sixth Avenues, the house that Mark Twain once lived in, and we walked out and wandered the streets of the Village on Sunday mornings and had brunch in Village restaurants, reading our paper over Bloody Marys. I was full of ambition, too much ambition, and worked my way up the organization of American Heritage, onto the staff of *Horizon* magazine, and up to the job of managing editor, to be the editor of the magazine. In the meantime we traveled to Europe and discovered the Italian Renaissance, and I wrote a few books about Renaissance figures, about Lorenzo de Medici and Erasmus and Pope Leo X and Luther. The amount we did is absolutely unimaginable and, my God, what was wrong with the flower children, after all? Of course it all came out badly, but at the time, the boys were in colorful clothes and the girls wore no bras and in beautiful weather it was indeed the springtime of life.

Yes, it all turned out to be much too wasteful. We were wasteful of ourselves and of each other, wasteful of booze, wasteful of pot, burned out by too much ambition, burned out by Vietnam and Lyndon Johnson and Richard Nixon, burned out by an excess of passion, both private and public.

I remember at the end of the 1960s, when I was the editor of *Horizon,* a poet friend of mine, David Rattray, who was working on the *Heritage Dictionary,* invited me to join him for lunch with an old friend of his named Vallee, who lived in Spain. Vallee was evidently a well-known Gypsy artist and famous character, whose house and, doubtless, bed, back in Spain was filled with dozens of different animals—dogs, cats, sheep, goats, bulls. I went up to David's office, and he offered me some marijuana. I took a few drags of a joint, and then Vallee came in. She was dressed in a bizarre costume, a skirt that went to the floor, a blouse of vaguely Indian derivation, and her face was painted like a stained-glass window. There is no doubt that she seemed to be a monstrous fraud, and yet she came into David's office very quietly and gently and said hello and took a couple of drags of the marijuana, sat down in David's chair and turned to me. I'd been standing there watching her, saying nothing. She turned to me and looked me full in the eyes and asked me very quietly, "What do you do?" And with that, I was suddenly, completely exhausted. I could not continue standing. I had to sit down. I felt as though my heart was going to stop, and as though I could not continue breathing.

On the way to lunch, going down in the elevator, Vallee stood at the back of the car, facing the door. As people got onto the elevator, they looked at Vallee, their eyes widened suddenly as they saw this peculiar vision standing in the elevator. They turned to face the front of the car, but gradually a smile would begin to work away at the corners of their mouths. They would try to suppress this smile. They would struggle with it. But they would not succeed. As the car went down from 21 to 20 to 19 to 18, these smiles grew and grew until finally all of the somber businessmen and

secretaries in the elevator began to titter and giggle
and chuckle, and soon enough they began to guffaw.
By the time the elevator reached the ground floor
and the doors opened, all the passengers came out
laughing. It was a wonderful ride.

But I could not go on with Vallee and David to
lunch. I was exhausted. I got a cab at the corner of
Forty-fifth Street and Fifth Avenue and went directly
back to my apartment. I could barely manage to get up
the stairs into the apartment. Each step was an
effort. I had to pull myself up, holding on to the
banister, sighing and groaning as I went. I felt all
of my vital processes were slowing down and would
finally cease to function. When I walked in the door,
Suzi was there, and she was horror-struck when she
saw me. I went to bed, and I lay there for two or
three days, I think. At the end of the third day, I
got up, I went to my office, I went to see the pub-
lisher, and I told him that I had to leave *Horizon*.
Later on, I would return to *Horizon* for a short period
of time. But, in essence, that was the end of *Horizon*
for me—and the end of the sixties.

Out of this miniature lifetime that finally burned
itself out, I am left, still alive, and with two beautiful
children. So I cannot see how the sixties can possibly
be despised. Nothing is happier than having children.
Nothing is more fun than having a chance to grow
up all over again. No love is sweeter or purer or
stronger, no matter how complex it may be or become, than that I feel for my children. And then

there are those extraordinary moments of discovery. I remember when my daughter, Erin, was only a couple of years old and we were up uncommonly early one morning, just before sunrise. It was at the end of summer. It was one of those brilliant warm summer days that just has the beginning tang of autumn in the air. We were in the country in a house in the woods near a lake. We dressed with sweaters, slacks, and sneakers and went down to the water where we got into a little sailboat and ghosted out onto the lake before anyone else was up and about. And we ghosted along silently over the clear water, out to where some ducks were swimming about. This was our plan, to move so quietly that we could come up and touch the ducks. We were not, of course, able to get close enough to touch the ducks before they flew away, but we came very close, and at first the ducks began to move quietly, swimming away from the boat. Then they moved a little more rapidly, and at last they took flight, and I watched my daughter as she looked very intently at the ducks flying away, and I had a sudden stupid realization that my daughter was laying away a quite-independent memory of her own, that suddenly she was no longer a baby, she was an independent, individual human being, and I was stunned.

And I remember when she first learned how to read. I was putting her to bed one night and reading her Mother Goose rhymes, when she corrected an error I made, and I asked her, because it seemed to me she was watching the words, if she was able to read. She looked somewhat bewildered and said she guessed she could. I asked her to read one of the other Mother Goose rhymes, and she read it. I was not sure whether or not she had memorized these rhymes, and so I asked her to read another and another, and still another. I was struck by the momentousness of this accomplishment, though she was quite calm. I began to seize easy-to-read books from the bookshelves near her bed and thrust one and then another into her hands, asking her to read this page or that page and calling out to Suzi, shouting, "Erin can read," and turning around, grabbing other books, thrusting them at Erin and shouting and raving like a madman, "You can read, you can read! Do you know that? You can read. Isn't that great? You can read," and finally calming down and saying to her very quietly, "Erin, that's wonderful. You can read," and she, smiling quietly, saying, "I know, Dad."

My son, Charles, was happy and bold from birth, bolder than I, and his smile is the smile of the sheer joy of life, which he had from the day of his birth. He lights up the room, and he gives pleasure wherever he goes. He will walk into a playground knowing no one, and within moments will be friends and playing with other boys and girls, both older and younger than he is. He is physically precocious, as I was, and, as I was, uninterested in intellectual matters. I identify with him utterly. I see my own childhood in him with a lucidity that is painfully sharp. I foresee his hurts and confusions and I have to catch myself to be sure I do not impose such self-fulfilling prophecies on him.

I cannot deny the sorrow. It is true that, for me, the disintegration of the nuclear family is not a curious abstraction. The breaking up of my marriage was a shattering, wounding, damaging, painful thing, for me, for my wife, for my children, and even now, if I permit myself to recall that time in all its details, I am overcome with confusion and exhaustion; I become heavy; I cannot move.

Now, I see my children often, two or three times a week, and sometimes for stretches of time; Suzi and I can speak with one another again; I can enjoy her again, admire her, like her, feel fond of her, love her, and miss her. Now, when we are together briefly from time to time with the children, I love it and am invigorated and even, strangely, content. But I do still miss the daily contact, the casual hugs, the kisses and hellos of my children.

I no longer—generous, understanding fellow that I am—attach all the blame for that broken marriage on Suzi. I was, among other things, the masochist in that marriage, provoking her rage and uncharitableness toward me by my drinking (among other things).

The sixties were full of rollicking good times, shouting and laughing, doing bizarre things in the middle of the streets, flaunting youth and vigor and beauty and brilliance and wit. But it was also not so funny. All writers are supposed to be big drinkers, and I did my stint in spades and found it amusing when I heard stories of Edmund Wilson habitually falling down in the Algonquin Hotel after an evening's conversation. And still, it is not so funny when you fall down in front of your frightened young children. It is not so funny when your mind is panicked by speed, made paranoid by marijuana, befuddled by booze, and you must then have an argument with your wife. It is not funny when the confusion leads to frustration and rage and then all that two beautiful grown young people are able to think to do is hit one another and scream and fall down.

I recall one nightmarish scene, as though out of a Hollywood movie. I had been given an award for the first book I wrote—something for youngsters about Lorenzo de Medici—and went to the small occasion arranged for the award, a cocktail party. I drank the obligatory drunken-poet, creative-genius-writer amount, insulted an editor (a small gesture in fuzzy-minded honor of Dylan Thomas), and left. Suzi and I were due to drive to the country that evening for the weekend. I arrived home to drive—drunk. Suzi and I and our three-year-old daughter in the car, on the West Side Highway out of Manhattan: Suzi asks if I would rather stay in town for the weekend; I, defensively, ask if Suzi would like to drive; she, passive-aggressively, says she only asked if I would like to stay in town for the weekend; the argument escalates. I pull off at 125th Street, get out of the car. Suzi follows. In the headlights of the car, as our child watches, Suzi knocks me down to the street. Cut.

Nor is it funny that two intelligent, sensitive, literate human beings were unable to see and cope with their problems until so much damage had been done that no marriage was left to repair. And yet, even so, I think that my marriage and the 1960s were alike, and I think I would say the same thing about both of them: I would have them both again.

And now, although my marriage is ended, and although I see my children often, still, when I am away, as during this time with Morgan in Washington, I miss them with a physical longing. But now I've forgotten Morgan, who is still talking—or maybe not. By now our conversation had become a sheer work of imagination, possibly all mine, possibly someone else's, but certainly not Morgan's alone, for sure.

MORGAN: There may have been a split within the intelligence community. A fight between factions, and the fight threatened to blow up and hurt some people. Colson said Hughes was the largest contractor for the CIA. Hughes gave Nixon a hundred thousand dollars. Hughes could blow Nixon out of the water. The rest of the Colson thesis is that Nixon was scared of Hughes, scared of the CIA. Now the CIA couldn't let Nixon talk, couldn't let him be put on trial. Who eased Nixon out of office? Haig? Is Haig a member of the CIA?

MEE: Are you telling me . . .

MORGAN: I'm not telling you anything. I'm asking questions.

MEE: Maybe the CIA pulled a coup.

MORGAN: Maybe the coup occurred long ago. There's not a military-industrial complex in this country. There's an intelligence-industrial complex. The CIA uses multinational corporations as fronts. To what extent does that prevent multinational corporations from regulation by the SEC and other regulatory bodies? The SEC gets to a certain point looking into a corporation, and the CIA may say: "OK, look fellows, you'll have to call this off." So you have an intelligence-industrial complex making national policy. You have covert actions, so you must have cover stories, cover-ups, credibility gaps. Lying is our national policy.

Thirty-five countries in the world have armies under contract from American corporations. Who has the war-making power in this country now? The President? Ask yourself this: When Nixon fired people, when he fired Haldeman and Ehrlichman, who did he replace them with? With national security people: Richardson, formerly on National Security Council, Haig, Buzhardt, formerly doing domestic security work at the Pentagon. Why? Ask Haldeman this: When Nixon went into the hospital with phlebitis, how come he said: "I'll never come out of the hospital alive"? What did he mean by that? Wanta have some lunch?

I was nervous about having lunch with the guy. Morgan had seemed perfectly sane during the im-

44

peachment campaign, but now, it seemed clear, his mind had snapped. Paranoia had driven him over the edge. He was raving. Questions and theories, suspicions and conspiracies went zinging around in Morgan's head in no particular order. It all refused to add up, and it sounded like the worst sort of Joe McCarthy wild charges, conspiratorial crackpot stuff, guilt by association.

Morgan and I were out on the street and into a day of false summer, wrongly warm, provocatively sunny. We turned and started walking up the Hill toward the Republican Club and restaurant. As we strolled up the Hill, I was struck by the way in which the Washington skyline had changed over the years. I had been a tourist in Washington twenty years before, when I was in my teens, and I remember, too, perhaps even more vividly, looking closely at the photographs of Washington that had been taken at the time of my childhood. When I was born, in 1938, the Capitol building dominated the Washington skyline. Tourists in Washington would gravitate to the mall, see the Washington and Jefferson monuments, then gaze up the mall to see that great monument to representative government, the Capitol. Behind the Capitol lay the Supreme Court, bastion of equal justice before the law. The President's house lay off this main axis as though the President were merely a functionary who carried out the obligations imposed by the will of the people and the law.

Today the Capitol no longer dominates Washington. Huge modern buildings, housing executive-branch agencies, swarm around the mall, creep up Capitol Hill, engulf the House and Senate. Washington architecture tells the story of American government in the past three decades: Political power has been drawn from the people, from local governments, from state governments, into Washington and, in Washington, into the executive branch. A swollen, sprawling, executive bureaucracy suffocates Capitol Hill.

Where are the congresspeople, the representatives of the people? They are to be found down underneath the office buildings, in the labyrinthine tunnels. The representatives of the people have gone underground.

I recalled something that Jack Newfield had written in *The Village Voice:* "Three weeks ago, many of the city's decent politicians held a joint press conference in Grand Central Station to oppose the increase in the transit fare to fifty cents. Ed Koch, Bella Abzug, Bob Abrams, Percy Sutton, Carol Bellamy, Franz Leichter, and Henry Stern, were all present.

"They were all freely elected by the people who live on the Lower East Side, in Co-op City, in Harlem, in Park Slope, in Throgs Neck, in Washington Heights, in Parkchester. But these elected officials reminded me of the early SDS students protesting the Vietnam War in 1965. They were right, but they were powerless. Although elected in a democracy, they assembled to get attention, just like the first war protesters."

Since World War II, Congress has voted away its

powers as fast as it possibly could. To be sure, nothing drains power from the people and the presumed representatives of the people faster and more certainly than a real, or invented, or a little bit real and a lot bit exaggerated external foe. Nothing kills a Republic quite as fast as a busybody foreign policy and its attendant arguments in favor of a strong executive. But, you cannot drain power from the Congress without its wholehearted cooperation, and what caused congresspeople to give up their constitutional powers was simple greed, stupidity, and meechiness.

Years ago, I was having dinner in the Market Inn in Washington. After dinner, I stepped outside to hail a taxi. As I stood there, a large black Cadillac limousine pulled up in front of the restaurant and before I had a chance to turn around to see who might be coming out of the Market Inn, the body of a woman hurtled past me and fell into the back seat of the car. She had obviously been pushed—a firm, swift, hard push in the small of the back, I would guess. I turned around and there was the Republican leader of the House of Representatives, beaming. And smashed. He was not for a moment flustered for having been caught in the act of sending his wife careering into the back seat of his limousine. On the contrary. He saw a new face. His right arm shot out, like an appendage of a giggling automaton, and he said, "Hello there, how are ya? I'm—" I suppress his name; he is no longer on the scene—"Good to see ya." He shook hands. "Nice night.

Beautiful day." Evidently he was not sure which it was. "Good to see ya. Nice to meet ya." And he stumbled on into the back seat of the limousine with his wife.

He was a man who loved his big limo and enough of the old spendola to pay for dinner at the Market Inn, to have the appearance of style and stature if nothing else; and he gave the impression of one who would do anything to keep his perquisites.

These guys develop a hunger and a need for the outward signs of honor in the same proportion, it seems, to which they toss away honor for the appearance of it, serving their party leaders and executive powerhouses. Their need for office, for respectability and recognition is deep and fierce. During the impeachment campaign, when I was in Washington trying to promote the idea that Congress should rise up and do its constitutional duty by tarring and feathering Nixon, I called on Representative Jack Brooks, a Democrat from Texas. He thought at first that I was a thug from the White House. The smoothy name for our committee, the National Committee on the Presidency, occasionally backfired, when our potential supporters took us for pretentious Nixonians. At that moment in the proceedings, impeachment politics had divided into Democrats versus Republicans, as though the issue were just one more in the same old ball game of log rolling, pork barreling, and citizen diddling.

"Don't you try to tell me how to vote!" Brooks said viciously, spitting and burning, holding up his

Democratic team, and looking utterly terrified and homicidal. "You go on back, and you tell your people that Jack Brooks is mean as a snake. Y'all hear me? Mean as a snake!"

Brooks was on my side then, and I liked what he said. Who knows? Perhaps he was not frightened of someone he took to be a Nixon thug; perhaps he was not even calculating the politics of the matter; perhaps he was simply honorably and courageously doing his constitutional duty. Who knows? But, it did occur to me that Brooks was a man who would do absolutely anything to hold onto the symbols of respectability and station and honor that his office meant—perhaps, sentimentally, since the time of his childhood—to him. He really was, beneath the terror and the insecurity, beneath the bluster and the pose of toughness, mean as a snake.

To an aide: "What? What do you mean my car is not theah? I told you five minutes ago I wanted my goddamn car ready, and I mean I want my goddamn car ready. I want it theah! Now you get your ass moving and you have that goddamn car present by the time I get down theah!"

The aide, face drained of all liquids, left at a run, with Brooks immediately behind him at a brisk pace, followed by briefcase-carrying assistant.

Nor do congresspeople much like to engage in real politics even when people weep and beg and parade in favor of the idea. During the Vietnam War, I was among the founders of a group that was started to make campaign material for antiwar congressmen. Our idea was to work for free for those candidates who could not afford Madison Avenue help. Our candidates had to be genuine, certifiable, grade-A doves, running against genuine, triple-A hawks. We found a few, and we made stuff for them, and all of our candidates—three of them—won. But the guy I remember most vividly is Lester Wolff from Long Island.

Wolff is a little rabbity fellow with a quick smile, bright eyes, a Bugs Bunny moustache, a nice guy. He wanted to stop the war, oh, how he wanted to stop the war: That was the issue, the one issue, the one and only issue that mattered; everyone knew it; it was the only issue on which the country wished to vote, the one on which citizens demanded a referendum, and it was the issue about which Lester Wolff's constituents cared, boy did they care, and did Lester ever intend to hit it hard. What did he intend to hit hard? The issue of ecology. Goddamn it, Lester was going to run on a platform of clean air and clean water, because that was what people really cared about on Long Island.

Hey, Lester, wait a minute; I thought they cared about the war.

Oh, yes, indeed they do. They care about that. But you wouldn't want to *run* on that issue. That is a *divisive* issue. What you need to win a campaign is an issue that *unites* people.

But, Lester, the whole point is to finally give the

poor fucking benighted people of America a chance
to express their views on the war. They've never had
a chance—except when they voted for Johnson against
Goldwater they thought they were voting against the
war, and when they voted for Nixon even a lot of them
thought they were voting against Johnson's war and
in favor of Nixon's secret plan to end the war, and
now, Lester, goddamn it, at last you've got to give
the fucking people a fucking chance in a fucking democracy to express their fucking will, do you know
what I mean, because that's the whole fucking point
of a democracy!

A long silence here: Look, I hate to say this, but I
don't think you understand politics.

So, that was Lester. So much for Lester. Both of
the other candidates avoided the issue of the war, too.
We helped them. They got in. They did vote against
the war, just as they said they would—privately. But
they made no issue of it. They all liked clean air and
clean water. We should have known. We should have
known when the issue of ecology came down the road,
when it was picked up by the politicians and cham-
pioned from every congressional district in America
that we were being had. How could it have escaped
us that this issue—like motherhood of old—was one
on which everyone would happily unite, the issue that
would smother all other, all real, issues. How could
we have fallen for it. God, how Lester and Hubert
and Dick and Spiro and all the boys must have been

laughing and scratching and chortling and rolling on the floor and buying another round on that one.

A tremendous amount of political intelligence is available to all of us all the time in our daily lives. We don't always notice it, and having noticed it and absorbed it, we don't usually realize that we've absorbed political information and that we are going to use it as the basis for political judgments and actions—but we have. We do this from birth, absorbing information we think has to do with mothers and fathers and brothers and sisters and playmates and schools and toys and allowance money—and only later realize it had to do with politics all along. Indeed, it is probably the best political information we have.

"The firmest and most general ideas I have are those which, in a manner of speaking, were born with me," wrote Michel Eyquem de Montaigne in his *Essays*, four hundred years ago, at the age of thirty-eight, my age. "Each man is a very good education to himself, provided he has the capacity to spy on himself from close up." And, in Montaigne's sense, we are all self-educated. In truth, a democracy depends upon this—that we learn not simply from books, from political philosophy, from Plato, from American history even, but that we learn from the bits and scraps of everyday life. It is that broad fund of daily experience on which the Republic draws for advice and consent to its destiny; if the aims of politicians can be ratified out of the collective wisdom, rational and irrational, of the daily lives of millions of people, then we have a better chance that those aims will be more or less suited to our survival as a nation and a species.

The course of politics must accord not merely with ideology, not merely with intellectual deductions, nor indeed only with passionately held urges—but with all those things at once: That is the strength of democracy that no other system of government can approximate. No other system has access to as much information about what is happening in the world, or as much direct touch with the things that need doing to nurture a good, continuing everyday life for the human species. So, what's gone wrong?

Morgan and I were both eating Caesar salads at the corner table in the Republican Club.

MEE: Look, if what you say is true, then who controls things? Who runs the country?

MORGAN: Beats me. Who chose Ford? Who was in on that decision? Did Nixon make it alone? Was it forced on him? Who chose Rockefeller? Beats me. I'm only saying this: This whole Watergate thing was very restricted. Many questions are left unanswered. We don't even have the tip of the iceberg. It is not a simple case. It has been made simple, clean, too neat.

The break-in is on June 17, 1972. OK, all Nixon cares about at first is getting reelected, that's all, a simple political matter. But, between June 17, 1972, and March 21, 1973, all sorts of things enter in—cover-ups, questions of CIA involvement, money traceable to illegal corporate contributions, all kinds of shit. Then, when it comes time for the Justice Department to frame a case on Watergate, they frame a case based exclusively on the events between March 21 and April 30, 1973: it is a very narrowly framed case. Very narrow. It embraces the cover-up, that's all. It's a big enough net to get a lot of people involved— small enough to leave out hundreds of questions. The Justice Department—Silbert, in fact, Nixon's man— frames the case: Cox follows that lead; Jaworski follows that lead; the House Judiciary Committee impeaches on that basis. I think the fix was in.

MEE: Who put the fix in?

MORGAN: You can't say it was one person. It suited the convenience of too many people. But essentially what it leaves out are all the lines going back to the CIA. That's all I'm saying.

MEE: Do you think Haldeman is CIA?

MORGAN: *No* [*lettuce suspended in midair*], I dunno [*lettuce falling off fork*], I doubt it [*fork back to the plate to retrieve the lettuce*], could be. He was what for J. Walter Thompson?

MEE: Los Angeles office manager.

MORGAN: Yeah. J. Walter Thompson may have been used as a CIA front. Someone at Thompson was an agent. I forget who.

MEE: Haldeman was the guy who suggested installing the taping system.

MORGAN: Yeah.

MEE: He destroyed Nixon.

MORGAN: Interesting.

Morgan and I returned to our salads, ordered

more iced tea, dessert, ice cream for Morgan, chocolate cake à la mode for me, hot coffee, black.

MEE: Do you think Haldeman is a double agent, working for Russia?

Morgan laughed—a rolling, jolly, thunderous, happy, pleased, belly-jiggling laugh.

According to the Morgan theory, then, we can imagine the following conversation that occurred during a crucial part of the eighteen-and-a-half-minute gap on the Nixon-Watergate tapes.

NIXON: Oh, hi, Bob. How are ya? What's up?

HALDEMAN: Well, we have this . . . uh . . . problem on the . . . uh . . . Watergate thing.

NIXON: Yeah.

HALDEMAN: Ehrlichman, Magruder . . . uh . . . Mitchell . . . and . . . uh . . . what's his name . . . Dean met yesterday and went over the whole ball of wax and . . . uh . . .

NIXON: Yeah.

HALDEMAN: It seems it was a CIA operation.

NIXON: Holy shit!

HALDEMAN: Yeah, that's what Mitchell said. Mitchell thought it was his operation—you know, find out what's going on at DNC like we talked about, you remember . . .

NIXON: Uh . . .

HALDEMAN: They want to know where O'Brien stands, with Mayhew or Hughes.

NIXON: Oh, yeah . . . uh-huh.

HALDEMAN: So there is this concern that all this

Hughes information will come out in an investigation. All the Hughes stuff with the CIA and other areas of national security concern.

NIXON: Right.

HALDEMAN: And also the Hughes thing . . . the money he gave Rebozo . . .

NIXON: What money?

HALDEMAN: The hundred thousand.

NIXON: Oh, yeah.

HALDEMAN: But the main worry is that all this is going to be traced to the White House.

NIXON: Why?

HALDEMAN: Because everyone here was involved up to their eyeballs.

NIXON: Oh, yeah.

HALDEMAN: So there's going to be a scandal for you.

NIXON: What does it have to do with me?

HALDEMAN: Mitchell says they did it on purpose.

NIXON: Who?

HALDEMAN: CIA.

NIXON: Oh, yeah, that's clear. They must have done it on purpose.

HALDEMAN: They got caught on purpose—to get you.

NIXON: What, me? Why?

HALDEMAN: They're taking over.

NIXON: Who is?

HALDEMAN: CIA.

NIXON: Now?

HALDEMAN: Right.

NIXON: Oh . . . one among us must be a betrayer.

HALDEMAN: Yes, sir.

NIXON: Who is it, Bob?

HALDEMAN: Mr. President, I don't know.

NIXON: Fuck 'em. They won't get me.

HALDEMAN: Mr. President, they've laid too much on you: the attempt on Castro, Kennedy's assassination, shooting Wallace . . . uh . . . Chappaquidick . . .

NIXON: How did I arrange Chappaquidick?

HALDEMAN: I can't tell you that.

NIXON: I'm beginning to get this . . . uh . . . you know, paranoid . . . uh, feeling that somebody, you know what I mean, is . . . uh . . . running this country.

HALDEMAN: I think that's just paranoid, sir.

NIXON: Just . . . uh . . . yeah, well . . . right. OK. Still, I get that feeling sometimes.

HALDEMAN: Yes, sir.

NIXON: I wish I knew who the hell it was.

HALDEMAN: [*posing as Jack Webb*] Well, I'll tell you this, Mr. President.

NIXON: Yeah?

HALDEMAN: It isn't you.

NIXON: Oh.

Two

ABOARD United Airlines Flight 799 to Los Angeles, my mind drifted. I was standing on a precipice, or a bluff overlooking the Pacific. The surf was up and angry, and the wind shrieked and bellowed, whipping bowed screens of sand up the curve of the bluff and across my face. Off to my left, on another bluff, separated from me by a range of smaller bluffs and gullies, stood Nixon, alone. I yelled out to him.

"Nixon!"

He did not hear me.

"Nixon!"

The sound traveled slowly; he turned slowly, his hunched shoulders coming round stiffly, tired and heavy. I yelled across the bluffs and gullies.

"I killed you!"

He looked at me silently.

"I killed you."

Finally, whether at last he heard, or at last he decided to answer for no reason at all, he called back, stupidly:

"What?"

"I killed you!"

A silence. Then, at last:

"Oh."

I searched for the right words, churning with rage.

"Stay dead, you shit!"

He gazed at me, not hearing. At last, uninterested, he turned away, cold, and looked out at the water.

We were flying over the Middle West, my home, the place where I was born, the heartland of Lincoln, Sandburg, Jesse James, Adlai Stevenson, Harry Ass Truman, home of liars, cheats, crooks, hypocrites, incompetents, and of egalitarianism, of populism, even of liberty.

The land of the Middle West rolls gently, is fertile, is lavishly watered by rivers and streams. To stand in the middle of the Middle West is to feel rich —richer by far than parsimonious easterners or pinched southerners can easily understand. To stand in the middle of the Middle West is to feel a part of inexhaustible wealth. It is exhilarating to sense the richness of the soil, the thickness of the grass, the casual generosity of the large shade trees. And the sheer size of the harvests of the Middle West, of the corn and the wheat and the other grain, is astounding.

I did not grow up on a farm, but I was certainly imbued with a sense of being surrounded by all of this natural plenty. I never saw a good reason for anyone to be uncomfortable, hungry, cold, badly clothed, sick, alone, or deprived in any way. If I saw any evidence that anyone was cold or hungry or uncomfortable, it puzzled me. Surely, one had only to go out in the fields and pick up a hoe to share in the abundant harvest. And if people did not pick up hoes, they must be lazy. If people somewhere don't have enough, someone must be lazy or something must be crooked, because anyone can see that there's plenty for those who work.

Now, we all know that this train of thought is nonsense. There simply is not enough in many parts of the world and in many parts of our own country for those who do want to work. Many people are unable to work. Many people are prevented from working. But when you ask a midwesterner to understand this, you are asking him to understand something that he is generally unable to perceive for himself and at the same time to deny the very powerful evidence of his own senses. We are all prisoners of the perceptions that come with the circumstances of our lives; hardly anyone entirely escapes that prison.

Political parties stand for nothing anymore, nothing but a joint, collusive grab for as much power as possible. But if parties did still stand for something—if the Democrats still did, for the most part, stand for the greatest possible social justice, even at the expense of a large federal government, and if the Republicans still did, for the most part, stand for maximum individual liberty, minimum government, even at the cost of social justice, then midwesterners would tend to be more Republican than Democrat.

In fact, of course, most midwesterners actually are Republican, as if party still did matter, as if pretending to believe made it so. They don't especially like choosing the Republican end of the stick; even at its best, they know that their founding fathers pledged them to liberty and justice, not liberty or justice, not liberty and maybe justice, if there is time and money. They, we, have not yet figured out how to have both ends of the stick, both liberty and justice. Most of us have despaired of an answer to this ancient dilemma— and the cop-out of the Midwest has been to come down on the side of individual liberty, of Republicanism, old-fashioned Republicanism, as though it still mattered. Midwesterners justify themselves, if at all, with Burke rather than Rousseau, with Hannah Arendt rather than John Rawls, with Robert Nisbet rather than Arthur Schlesinger.

So you pays your money. Most midwesterners have come down on one side of the dilemma, many of the rest of us on the other. They aren't any happier than we are, as far as I can figure. They pretend they are, but, in truth, all they are is a little more defensive about it.

In my own family there have been both Republicans and Democrats, both Tories and rebels, and I take a kind of perverse pride at the wonderfully wild, generally unpruned look of my family tree. The English historian, J. H. Plumb, has said that all living English men and women are direct descendants of William the Conqueror—thus, a plumby back of the hand at genealogical pretensions. Still, Plumb alone cannot keep me from being genealogically pretentious, and I trace my ancestry, by way of exquisitely judicious and ruthless pruning of the family tree, back to Thomas Hutchinson, the governor of Massachusetts, who sided with the Tories against the rebels and helped bring about the Boston Tea Party. Good old Uncle Thos.

Hutchinson was himself related to Anne Hutchinson, the first woman to play a leading role in American history, according to Samuel Eliot Morrison. She was a witch. Not exactly a witch: Anne Hutchinson, born in England in 1591, emigrated in 1634 to Massachusetts Bay, where, in her new home, she "interpreted" the sermons of John Cotton for groups of friends and acquaintances. She became a preacher, at a time when virtually no one else in America questioned the assumption that woman's place was in the home, and, what was possibly even worse, she preached that salvation came through an individual's awareness of the grace of God (the "covenant of grace"), not through faithful subservience to the laws of church and state (the "covenant of works"). Carried to its logical extreme, Anne Hutchinson's theology provided a rationale for her followers to disobey all laws of church and state, or, at the very least, to dissent most vigorously. Anne Hutchinson's theology could presumably justify both Richard Nixon and the Weathermen. The governors of Massachusetts Bay banished Anne Hutchinson in 1637. The difficulty she posed for the new colonies led ultimately to the promulgation of the principle of religious liberty and to the separation of church and state, the foundation upon which all other American liberties were built. Anne moved on to Long Island, where she settled next to a river that now bears the Hutchinson name, and where, in 1643, she and her family were massacred by Indians.

Thomas Hutchinson was born in Boston some generations later, in 1711. He was appointed lieutenant governor of Massachusetts in 1758, chief justice in 1760, governor in 1770. He had opposed the Sugar Act of 1764 and the Stamp Act of 1765; but, for all his disagreements with the policies of the British government, he remained a Loyalist. "We don't live in Plato's Commonwealth," he said, "and when we can't have perfection, we ought to comply with the

measure that is least remote from it." An intelligent
man, a thoughtful man, a learned man, Hutchinson
did not quite understand what political liberty meant
—else he would not have used Plato's Commonwealth
as his notion of perfection. He said it was wrong—in
fact, he said it was unconstitutional—for Britain to
tax the American colonies; but he said that if Parliament chose to tax the colonies, then "it is more ad-
visable to Submit to it, than by resistance to break of
the Connection."

"Hutchinson also indulged," Morrison tells us,
"in a newspaper debate with Samuel Adams and his
friends on constitutional principles. Both drew freely
on ancient history and Latin and Greek literature.
This was most imprudent on the Governor's part,
because not only did Adams put it over on him in
classical learning; he drove him into a corner, where
he had to admit that Americans had no rights other
than those that King and Parliament chose to recognize."

Hutchinson's heavy-handed attempts to enforce
the law that gave the British East India Company a
monopoly on the sale of tea in America led to the
Boston Tea Party in 1773. Hutchinson concluded that
matters had reached such a state that only military
action could restore law and order to the colonies;
and so, with a final recommendation that the military
be called in to solve the colonial problem, Hutchinson departed his native country and went to England
in 1774, where he settled down on a farm, like

Richard Nixon in San Clemente, and waited for the dust to settle so that he could return to Boston. He died on June 3, 1780, never having comprehended the American Revolution, thinking he was right.

Sophia Hoppin of Rhode Island was descended from Thomas Hutchinson. In the middle of the nineteenth century, Sophia Hoppin took the train to Omaha. She wore black silk, a starched, lacy blouse, black silk hat full of stick pins, mother of pearl, bits and blobs and rings of gold, a formidable woman, buxom and robust, with a firm and elevated jaw, and calm, commanding eyes. Jesse Lowe, her groom-to-be, met her at the train station in Omaha and put his Hoppin fiancée in a wheelbarrow and wheeled her through the muddy streets of Omaha to their new home.

Jesse Lowe, my great-grandfather, was a founder and the first mayor of Omaha. He was a tough old man, a pioneer in starched white collar and rolled-up sleeves, shooting coyotes on the streets of his new town, whacking it out with bank robbers, living with Indians. I am that close to the frontier, as any midwestern boy is. My uncle was shot dead on the street in Omaha by bank robbers. On my fireplace hangs the head of a bobcat, shot by another uncle in midtown Omaha. Somewhere around the house is an Indian tom-tom, made of buffalo hide and bent wood—not painted, but plain, utilitarian, a business tom-tom, for sending ominous messages. And laid carefully away in a drawer is a disintegrating, lavishly beaded

Indian medicine bag, with a few bits of dried herb at the bottom. It is this medicine bag, so my grandmother Nan told me, that was among the prizes offered by the Indian chief for my infant mother. Who knows? Nan also maintained that Omaha was originally called Lowemaha in honor of Jesse.

It is from my mother's mother that most of these stories of my family come. I believe that the first word I ever knew how to spell, as I think back on it, must have been Nan, because, as children eternally discover to their delight, it is spelled the same way both forward and backward.

It was Nan who put me to bed so many nights when I was a child and told me bedtime stories while she scratched my back. She lived into her eighties, this wonderful woman, and I can still remember most vividly the softness and delicacy, and translucence, even, of her skin, of her very quiet, very calm, very warm and utterly direct eyes. I remember her blouses of silk with lace cuffs and lace collars and cascades of lace coming down the front of her bodice. She told me of her family's history, my family's history, of the past, of the way life used to be in the Middle West. She told me stories of Indians of the plains, of the Indian chief who had once tried to trade that old medicine bag and swatches of wampum for the papoose who was my mother—for Nan was, at times, one of the greatest galloping liars that the Middle West ever produced. She told me of having known Mark Twain when she was a child, and that is at least possible, since Twain and Nan's family came from the same part of the country and were all involved in politics at roughly the same time. She told me of having been dandled on the knee of Thomas Alva Edison. In short, she civilized me. She placed me and my life in the context of the rest of the world of past, present, and of expectations for the future.

And, as I look back on it, she had republicanism in her bones, in a way that would have made old Jefferson proud, and she spoon-fed it to me day and night. Consider the simple republican elegance of the story of Jesse Lowe. Jesse got together with some friends and started a town. The town needed a mayor. Jesse served. Then he stepped aside and someone else became mayor of Omaha. It is a great marvel that this new town was not called Cincinnati.

This is, as Nan obviously meant it to be, the very model of the American politician: He does his civic duty, and, having done it, he returns to private life. Alexis de Tocqueville was not more eloquent than Nan.

"There are," Tocqueville wrote in the nineteenth century of *Democracy in America,* "in all, nineteen principal offices in a township. Every inhabitant is required, on pain of being fined, to undertake these different functions, which, however, are almost all paid, in order that the poorer citizens may give time to them without loss." This was, in truth, government by the people: All people were expected to participate and serve in the public arena.

70

Municipal institutions, Tocqueville said, "constitute the strength of free nations. Town meetings are to liberty what primary schools are to science; they bring it within the people's reach, they teach men how to use and how to enjoy it. A nation may establish a free government, but without municipal institutions it cannot have the spirit of liberty. . . .

"In the township," Tocqueville says, "as well as everywhere else, the people are the source of power; but nowhere do they exercise their power immediately. In America the people form a master who must be obeyed to the utmost limits of possibility." A citizen "obeys society, not because he is inferior to those who conduct it or because he is less capable than any other of governing himself, but because he acknowledges the utility of an association with his fellow men and he knows that no such association can exist without a regulating force. He is a subject in all that concerns the duties of citizens to each other; he is free, and responsible to God alone, for all that concerns himself. Hence arises the maxim, that everyone is the best and sole judge of his own private interest, and that society has no right to control a man's actions unless they are prejudicial to the commonweal or unless the commonweal demands his help. This doctrine is universally admitted in the United States."

We have changed so drastically since the days of Tocqueville and Jesse Lowe that it is a pleasure just to listen to them talk, just to recall what clarity and freshness once characterized people's heads. Here is

71

another small hunk of Tocqueville just for the hell of it:

"Granting, for an instant, that the villages and counties of the United States would be more usefully governed by a central authority which they had never seen than by functionaries taken from among them; admitting, for the sake of argument, that there would be more security in America, and the resources of society would be better employed there, if the whole administration centered in a single arm—still the *political* advantages which the Americans derive from their decentralized system would induce me to prefer it to the contrary plan. It profits me but little, after all, that a vigilant authority always protects the tranquility of my pleasures and constantly averts all dangers from my path, without my care or concern, if this same authority is the absolute master of my liberty and my life, and if it so monopolizes movement and life that when it languishes, everything languishes around it, that when it sleeps, everything must sleep, and that when it dies, the state itself must perish . . . when a nation has arrived at this state, it must either change its customs and its laws, or perish; for the source of public virtues has dried up, and though it may contain subjects, it has no citizens."

Jesse Lowe served. In that respect, and that alone, he was the archetypal American politician. In all other respects, he could—as far as the system cares— have been a reprehensible character, personally rotten, the very picture of degradation compared to

Thomas Hutchinson. We do not know what fantasies the first mayor of Omaha may have had about savaging savages or bedding down with Indian maidens. I often fantasize about Indian maidens, and I have only once ever met one. For all we know, Jesse Lowe was a wheelbarrow fetishist. It is a central characteristic of the American political system that a wheelbarrow fetishist could be mayor of Omaha. Americans are only American in public, as public men and women, in public spaces, performing public duties. In private, we may all be wheelbarrow fetishists, and the system does not care. Nor should we. Do we worry because a man's finger is on the nuclear trigger? The solution is not to worry, not to become preoccupied with gossip about court life, but to take away his kingly life-and-death power and leave him to his bizarre sexual practices with wheelbarrows, as we would have him leave us to our private lives.

My family trickled to America on almost every boat that fetched up on the New World's shores, beginning with the *Mayflower* and floundering through the nineteenth century, with Germans who moved on to St. Louis, some Welsh, some Irish, some French, some Scots, some lowborn scum and some highborn haughties, Protestants and Catholics, atheists and deists.

My father's father, William Louis Mee, with his three-piece suit and his gold watch chain, materialized from England in San Francisco, not having heard, perhaps, that the gold rush was over. He brought with

CHARLES L. MEE, JR.

him his crimson jacket with brass buttons that he had
worn as a fencing instructor in the Goldstream
Guards, a single medal he had won in a fencing competition, and a beautiful, carved meerschaum pipe,
and he never talked of his childhood, so unhappy it
must have been. He did not enjoy talking about his
past, or his origins, but I think I know what they
were. The name Mee is a very ancient and very rare
Irish name. By rights, my grandfather should have
come from Ireland. He came, instead, from England
and, more particularly, from the area around Manchester. Manchester, as it happens, was a town to
which many of the Irish fled during the years of the
great potato famine in the nineteenth century. So my
grandfather's father, or grandfather, must have been a
refugee from starvation. The wealthy Irish were not
refugees from starvation. The refugees from starvation were the poor, despised dirt farmers. The English
regarded them as a lazy, rotten shiftless bunch. And,
when they began to starve, the English government
regarded the Irish as a willful nuisance. The English
regarded the Irish in much the same way that many
Americans regard those who live on welfare. And so,
when the Irish began to starve, the English were not
immediately sympathetic, even though of course Ireland was a part of Great Britain. What followed in
the 1840s and on into the 1850s has been called by
some genocide; it has been called genocide not merely
by starving Irish but also by some of the Englishmen
who were charged with administering the apparently

74

purposely inadequate relief plans. Estimates vary a great deal, but in the end, the Irish population was reduced during the famines of the 1840s—by way both of emigration and death—by about 30 percent. "I have always felt a certain horror of political economists," Benjamin Jowett said at the time, "since I heard one of them say that he feared the famine . . . would not kill more than a million people, and that would scarcely be enough to do much good." This, then, is my grandfather's heritage—and mine.

He was a great gentleman, my grandfather, with his thin white hair and silver-rimmed, octagonally shaped glasses that shone like polished crystal, his deliberate manner, his reserve, his dignity, his aloofness. When he came to visit on Sundays, for Sunday dinner, I remember nothing of his arrival (doubtless I was out playing?), nothing of sitting at the table for dinner itself, nothing of the presence of my father's mother. But I do remember the time after Sunday dinner, when it seemed as though whole rooms were swept aside, cleared from my grandfather's path so that he could make his stately progress to the largest and most commandingly positioned chair in the living room. He was a modest man; he did not aspire to patriarchal grandeur, but he accepted the role, and he could fill it. He would sit quietly, fixing his meerschaum pipe, and a cup of tea would be brought to him, making those wonderful bell-like clattering and tinkling sounds of delicate china and silver. And, as he settled back and took an appreciative sip of tea and replaced the cup on his saucer, that is the moment at which I would present myself to him. He hadn't the foggiest idea what to do with me. He did not know how to talk to me: what does a small—five- or six- or seven-year-old—child enjoy discussing? He was too stiffly Edwardian to reach forward and give me a bear hug. He did not know what to do. So he would begin circling his forefinger in great arcs through the air and buzz like a bee; the finger would trace ever smaller circles until, at last, the bee would zero in to buzz directly into the middle of my tummy. And I would laugh and giggle and chortle and laugh and fall rolling on the floor, helplessly giggling and squealing, and I would get up again at last and go back again for more, and my grandfather would send me laughing and rolling to the floor again and again and again. That was our game; that was what we had to say to one another; and we loved to say it over and over again to one another of a Sunday afternoon, until we were both exhausted, and then on another Sunday we would resume, saying the same thing over and over to one another, and we spoke to each other again and again in this way. He could make me laugh until I ached, my grandfather could, and make me ache still today when I think back on it and recall that feeling in my stomach.

Yet, clearly, it will not work, this family that came to America to be free and equal—for the French hate the Welsh, and the Irish hate the Scots, and I am not sure myself how I feel about the Germans. But apparently it did work; it worked politically. What all of these people have in common, what makes them all Americans, is politics and nothing else. They share the public space as free and equal citizens. That, and only that, is what makes Americans Americans.

That is our special blessing, and our special curse. The French without politics are still French, the Germans still Germans, the Italians still Italians; but if the American Republic dies, the American people are disoriented; they are no longer who they thought they were; they cannot know who they are; they are no longer quite Americans; when the Republic dies, the people die, and that is why, for us, politics is so important and why, when politics goes berserk, we all go mad.

All else that we have in common, all of the national traits we share, come from the fact that we exist, as Americans, politically. The American melting pot evidently did not work sociologically. We have not all left our ghettos; we have not all intermarried, we have not all lost our ancestral traits and traditions—and a fine thing that certainly is. But the melting pot does work as a political entity, and it may be a part of our present national catastrophe that we tend to think sociologically these days and have forgotten how to think politically.

I dream on this vision aboard flight 799 to Los Angeles: To wit, viz., a capsule history of the United States, thus, in twenty-five words or less: since WWII, power has flowed out of state and local governments to central government, to federal government, and within federal government, to executive branch. Aha! But why, we may well ask, did the Founding Fathers design a government with federal, state, and local separations, as well as executive, congressional, and judicial checks and balances? Good question. Do I see a hand? Anyone? Yes.

So that power would be so widely distributed that no one could find the one single place where power was and grab it.

Excellent! Proceed.

Thus, in the nineteenth century in the days of Alexis de Tocqueville and Jesse Lowe, Tammany Hall could be corrupt. Or the Pennsylvania legislature could be so corrupt that reformers could say of it: "Standard Oil has done everything with the Pennsylvania legislature except refine it. . . ."

[*Laughter*]

As time went on, power tended to reside more and more in the hands of the oligarchs, the political bosses, and the rich. But still, and even so, as long as all power was not concentrated in one place, one level or branch, the system could cleanse itself, right itself, let free democratic principles ooze back into it from the federal government or the local government or from a free press.

Good.

Ideally, of course, power would be so widely distributed that an equal chunk of power would reside in the hands of each individual citizen. This is the idea of pure democracy. Its virtue is obvious: In this way, if power is so very widely distributed, it is impossible for any thief to grab it all. In our system, we compromise with that principle—though, as we have learned, the more we compromise with it, the more the oligarchs take over and the riskier it is that some rotten bastard two-faced, son of a . . . .

That will do.

. . . that some power-crazy politician will try to take it all.

Indeed.

Indeed. After WWII, power became concentrated in the hands of the President. Everyone, it seemed, wanted it this way: ambitious pols who wanted power, businessmen who wanted profits, labor leaders who wanted clout. And the rest of us put up with it, acquiesced, believed it right—in the cause of uniting against the Common Foe in the Cold War.

Ahhh. Alas.

Alas, yes, and, yet again, alas. For suddenly everyone saw where the power was.

Of course.

Of course, yes, but also alas. For, it had become visible, this power. Too visible. For, once you can see it, you can steal it.

I see.

Schlesinger was right, but there is more to the story: As the Imperial presidency became stronger, it

also became weaker. As power was increasingly concentrated in the office of the President, it became increasingly vulnerable. . . .

To?

To rip-offs. And thus you arrive at today, where
everyone is trying to rip it off—multinationals, the
CIA, bankers, the Pentagon, the armaments com-
panies, foreign countries, Mafia mobsters. The oligarchs are fighting among themselves now, and it has
nothing to do with us anymore, with the Republic.
We are only spectators now, watching the longest-
running continuous palace revolution of churning
coups and countercoups now playing in any stadium
in the world. And so the Oval Office, source of rigidity
and repression in America, possible source of tyranny,
is, at one and the same time, the source, too, of
anarchy!

My God!

And because, do you see, because the thing that has
so disoriented the system is the concentration of power
in the Oval Office, then the more the President tries
to bring order to the system, so much more will he
bring disorder to it, the more he tries to discipline it,
he will create anarchy just that much more.

"Kings and governors," Sam Adams said in 1771,
"may be guilty of treason and rebellion; and they have,
in general, in all ages and countries, been more frequently guilty of it than their subjects. Nay, what has
been commonly called rebellion in the people has often
been nothing else but a glorious struggle in opposition

to the lawless power of rebellious kings and princes."

"Beautiful."

Who spoke?

The man sitting next to me on the airplane, a man who reminded me of my father, a business executive no doubt, in gray pinstripe suit, silk rep stripe tie, button-down white Brooks Brothers shirt, charcoal-gray soft wool socks, black brogans—the uniform. He was a pleasant man, in his early sixties (my father is in his seventies), with distinguished gray hair (like my father's), well tanned (perhaps a golfer, like my father), an easy, confident smile, slightly condescending to the younger man, signifying that he has had many years' practice in a solid executive position; he is accustomed to being the one who does the accepting and the rejecting. I look at him, bewildered.

"Beautiful view."

I looked out the window. We were, by this time, past the Rockies and flying out over the powder pastels of the desert that undulates west to Las Vegas and Los Angeles. It was a beautiful view, and I was moved by it, but still distracted by my daydreams. Suddenly I came out of my reverie and focused on him.

"You're a businessman."

"Yes, I'm with Exxon."

It was not my father after all, but the enemy face to face! It occurred to me at once that here was an opportunity to get to know a genuine fascist bastard, not a trimming or decent businessman but a real rotter, and

to hear at first hand those hollow public relations eva-
sions, how corporate crime is an unfortunate quirk, an
exception to the good, public spirited ways of American
business in general, how liberals and Commies should
not tear down the structure that makes America work
and produces a higher standard of living for blah, blah,
blah. I had gone this far. I might as well proceed—
carry on my mad political dream with this, my newfound interlocutor.

"What do you think the problem is?"

"What problem?"

"For democratic governments."

A moment's pause only.

"They're a pushover."

"How do you mean?"

"They're corrupt, administered by incompetent,
selfish, and generally ignorant politicians. They're
out of contact with the real world. Many of them are
simply irrelevant these days—or relevant only as a
nuisance to the present governments of the world."

"The present governments?"

"I exaggerate." Exxon smiles, takes a Pall Mall
from a silver case, offers one to me. I take it, produce
a match. Exxon settles back in his seat.

"Increasingly, it seems to me, multinational corporations are becoming the effective governments of
the world. Why not? It is not written in heaven that
the nation-state is the eternal form for political institutions. The nation-state has not existed forever—nor,
for that matter, been an unadulterated blessing for the

world. The city-state did not last forever. The Holy Roman Empire did not last forever. New political institutions constantly grow up, replace old, worn-out institutions."

MEE: Are they worn out, or are you killing them?

EXXON: [*with a smile*] Are you accusing me of corrupting governments?

MEE: Yes.

EXXON: Well, sure, of course that's true. But you're being too simplistic. First of all, if the nation-state can't defend itself, perhaps it deserves to be corrupted to death. Politicians don't define real issues for the country, give the electorate a real choice. They are not accountable to the people; there's no connection anymore between politicians and the people; so there is simply no legitimacy left in government. Most governments these days are simply illegitimate. Ours is not a legitimate government. So, the Republic is dying—or dead.

MEE: You killed it.

EXXON: Well, look, politicians do not govern. Governments do not effectively govern. If you have a power vacuum, someone will move into it. Multinationals have moved into the vacuum. Maybe there's some virtue in it. Multinationals have to be responsive to some sort of reality, to the reality of economics, the reality of profit and loss statements, to the making and distribution and consuming of things. There is a widely shared belief in the world that such things constitute reality. There is not a widely shared belief in the world that American liberties have any reality. So multinationals give you a system of government that refers to a common sense of reality. That's what will work; whether it is, in point of fact, real or not.

MEE: And this, speaking generally, is the way in which oligarchy is established.

EXXON: What's that?

MEE: And this, speaking generally, is the way in which oligarchy is established.

ADEIMANTUS: Yes; but what are the characteristics of this form of government, and what are the defects . . . ?

SOCRATES: First of all, consider the nature of the qualification. Just think what would happen if pilots were to be chosen according to their property, and a poor man was refused permission to steer, even though he was a better pilot?

ADEIMANTUS: You mean that they would shipwreck?

SOCRATES: Yes; and is not this true of the government of anything?

ADEIMANTUS: I should imagine so.

SOCRATES: Except a state?—or would you include a state?

ADEIMANTUS: Nay, the case of a state is the strongest of all, inasmuch as the rule of a state is the greatest and most difficult of all.

SOCRATES: This, then, will be the first great defect of oligarchy?

ADEIMANTUS: Clearly.

SOCRATES: And here is another defect that is quite as bad.

ADEIMANTUS: What defect?

SOCRATES: The inevitable division: Such a State is not one, but two States, the one of poor, the other of rich men; and they are living on the same spot and always conspiring against one another.

ADEIMANTUS: That, surely, is at least as bad.

SOCRATES: . . . And there may be many other evils.

ADEIMANTUS: Very likely.

MEE: So, I oppose it.

EXXON: So I see.

MEE: And you see its defects—evils, perhaps—and yet you support it, thus finally assuring that America shall have neither liberty nor justice.

EXXON: Look, there's no point in kicking against the inevitable.

MEE: You're a Marxist, hunh?

EXXON: What's that?

MEE: You're a Marxist. Marx was a historical determinist. You are a historical determinist. Therefore, you are a Marxist.

EXXON: Very interesting. Syllogistically defective, I think, but interesting.

The plane landed in Los Angeles.

As we taxied in toward the terminal, Exxon turned to me and spoke quietly: "See here, I gather you're irritated, but open your mind a moment. You know that the nation-state had to be invented centuries ago and that, when it was, it was not a beautiful thing to behold. The liberties that you cherish had to be forced down the nation-state's throat. But, once they were, the nation-state was not all bad. We got a lot of use out of it. It did a lot to improve the world.

"So stop fighting the multinational corporate state for just a moment. Think of it. Regard it as the coming thing. Then, what must you do? First, you must write constitutions for these corporations. You must get the employees to behave like citizens of their corporations. Capitalism as we have known it is totally dead. None of these multinational corporations have anything to do with capitalism anymore. Have you read *The Juggernauts* by Graham Bannock? Read it. The original owners disappeared years ago. Corporations are left with managers. Read Galbraith. And the first job of managers, often, as they themselves see it, is not to produce anything or make profits, but to provide jobs. Don't you see? These corporations are already behaving more like nations than businesses. The employees should own them. Read what's his name, Louis Kelso. That's first. Employee ownership. And constitutions.

"Think of it. You'd have a whole array of new nations. And the social contract would be a literal reality for once, not merely a rhetorical device. Different corporate-nations would offer different social contracts to their citizens. You could move from citizenship in one corporation to citizenship in another. Would you prefer to have no set of rights and obligations at all, no demands on your service, and no fringe benefits for you? No duties to perform, no protection from the state? Fine. You opt out. You work for no corporation. You live in a state of nature. You see? All that would be possible all of a sudden.

"And what happens to the old nation-states? They stay. They continue. Why not? For a few centuries anyhow. They become increasingly like churches. At first they have some political power. Gradually they lose it. They retain a sort of moral force. People would, naturally, have sentimental attachments to different nations. You'd have to arrange for freedom of allegiance to different nations. And the nation-state would still be able to collect some taxes. Not as much as now. But some. A tithe. That's all. A tithe. This tithe would pay for charities, such as welfare. No longer would anyone object to welfare ever again—at least not for a century or two. It would be removed from politics. It would become, again, as it should be, as it is, as it has always been, a moral matter, not a political matter. You see?"

"And if unions set up rival states," I offer, "then you'll have rival nations of the haves and the have-nots."

"No, no. The unions can never be nations. They have no property. If you want to have a nation, you must have turf; you must have property to stand on. Yes, it will be rich against poor. Rich multinationals against poor, disorganized Africans, Indians. But not against unions. The unions have already sold out.

Unions are just goon squads. Don't worry about them."

The plane had arrived at the terminal. My traveling companion was all brisk readiness. He seized his briefcase, leaped to his feet, smiled.

"I enjoyed talking to you."

We shook hands. I never caught sight of him again in the terminal. But now I knew: At last I had met a real radical, and not just some cheap, unshaven imitation.

I looked for him in the baggage area. On second and third thought, I had some questions I wanted to put to him. I poked around through the crowd, but I couldn't find him. I did find Harold Lasswell, however, the white-haired professor emeritus of Yale, formerly University of Chicago, practicing political scientist and psychiatrist, a mandarin who, when asked a question, purses his lips, clears his throat, and hums.

Hi, how are ya?

Hmmm. Yes, how are you?

Fine. What are you doing here?

Hmmm. Yes, I am going to participate in a seminar. Hmmm. And you?

I'm going to see H. R. Haldeman. Remember Haldeman?

Hmmm. Yes, Haldeman. An interesting specimen —of what I'm not sure.

Lissen, Harold, I was just talking with this guy who says the multinationals are going to be the new governments of the world. What do you think of that?

Harold found one of his suitcases.

Hmmmm.

Izat true?

Hmmm.

He found another suitcase.

Izit?

Mmm. That's rather passé. I think it far more likely that we shall see the evolution of a world oligarchy, an open oligarchy rather than a closed or restricted one, open on the basis of merit and . . . mmm . . . loyalty, drawing its members interchangeably from among the elites of the United States, Russia, and China.

Are you serious?

Mmmm.

That's the final end of democracy, huh? That's the price we pay for losing it hmmm?

Mmmm.

Harold, the oligarchs—will they be nice guys?

Hmmm.

Then Harold vanished, too, and I was left alone in dreadful, stinking Los Angeles, that great, putrid sprawl of exhaust fumes and ticky tack, weird, sickly green tuberous plants, grotesquely large as though cancerous, a cancerous city, a city without a center, a five-and-ten-cent city, mecca of shoddy, Potemkin town, fountainhead of unctuousness and tartuffery, quackery and lies, sham and falsehood, home of the bogus and spurious, home of the smooth and sniveling, home of the glib and the two-faced, home of the bland and the fake; it made me sick.

Nonetheless I got as far as the Beverly Wilshire Hotel. The sunshine, even through the smog, even though diffused, was too bright, as though the sky were lit by banks of fluorescent tubes. The air was sickeningly warm and thick with Pacific viscidity. I felt unwell, no doubt of that. I felt light-headed; I felt woozy and befuddled from the plane trip, I felt confused and somewhat homesick. I needed a shower and a chance to lie down for a few minutes. I checked in to the hotel distractedly and followed the bellhop to the elevator and to the room where once again I was left alone. I was beginning to feel consistently abandoned.

Then, it seemed to me that something was wrong. I was standing in the middle of a garret room at the top of the Beverly Wilshire Hotel. It was not clear that anything was in fact and beyond doubt wrong. But something seemed so. What seemed particularly wrong at the moment was that I had the distinct feeling that I was in danger. I had the feeling that I was being bugged—or watched.

This feeling of being bugged or watched, the thought of having had my privacy violated, led quickly to thoughts of violations of other privacies, to fantasies akin to rape and buggery. I felt exposed. This impression was followed by a sudden rushing to the head of feelings of fears of enjoyment.

All this bears thought, not to say analysis. There is rich material here for talk of sexual fantasies, both normal and abnormal, but, even more, here is a hint of fantasies more depraved than those of sex, more embarrassing to admit to in our times than the most embarrassing Victorian deviations. Here is a hint of fantasies (again) of power.

And yet, this was no time to indulge in hours or days of catatonic self-analysis. I had work to do. It was time to get on with it. And so, just in case, just to be on the safe side, I took the following precaution: I called the front desk and requested a room change.

Actions galvanize perceptions. While the phone rang, I looked around the room once more. This room in which I had been placed was a small and meanly furnished room at the top of the hotel. Its carpet was threadbare. Its walls seemed insubstantial. The bed-spread seemed old and dusty—tattered. The bulb in the bedside lamp was burned out. The room was at the end of the corridor, dimly lit. The corridor was accessible only by way of a single elevator, the hotel staff's elevator. The entire arrangement was reminiscent of that enjoyed by Sir Hugh Fitzhugh in the Tower of London.

We walked in stately fashion, the bellhop and I, down the dimly lit corridor, back to the staff elevator —he in the lead with the bags, I two steps behind, like a shah or pasha and his porter. At the elevator, the two of us stood silently maintaining our distance, and I felt put down by him. There was no question, whatever our master-slave relationship, he was the one who was in charge of his emotions. The elevator ride was chastening, too. I suffered under the silent judgment of the elevator operator. I felt like the small boy who had gone out to the end of the high dive and was unable to jump, now climbing back down the ladder.

We stopped at the eighth floor, and this miniature parade, with fleeting hallucinations of elephants and other pack animals, disembarked and made its grand paranoid progress to room 832. The bags were set down, the bellhop tipped, the door quietly and firmly closed. I was again alone.

Ensconced in my new room, it was then that the full subtlety of the plan dawned on me. The spies, the CIA, the FBI, whoever they were, had anticipated that I would insist upon being moved from that mean little room. Of course, they would have known that I wouldn't stay in a room where the light bulb was burned out in the bedside table lamp. If anything, they had made it too obvious. It was clear that the room that had been bugged was this room, the new room, room 832. I stood, transfixed, in the midst of room 832, thinking calmly.

After a while, I was standing, thinking, next to the desk on which the phone sat.

At some point, one must wonder whether these feelings of paranoia are realistic or not, derived from the external world in which we live, or the internal world we project outward.

I was sitting on the edge of the bed in room 832 of the Beverly Wilshire Hotel, thinking about calling H. R. Haldeman.

I was sitting with the phone at hand, on the edge

of the bed in room 832, looking out the window over the shops and boutiques and snug houses of Beverly Hills.

Now this sort of thing, this distracted daydreaming can go on only so long before complete stasis sets in and, whatever the cause, one's self-image becomes that unacceptable picture of stark staring (ever so quiet) madness. One must plunge ahead at moments like this, tossing off quick brave phrases such as who knows? and who cares? and devil-take-the-hindmost, and what is truth? Thus I picked up the phone and dialed Haldeman's home. Haldeman himself answered. His first word on the phone was, I thought, fiendishly clever, a tour de force of the noncommittal. He said:

"Hello."

I introduced myself. He was glad to hear from me, glad to know I was in town, had had a good trip, was able to get together. I suggested lunch the day after tomorrow. That sounded fine to him. I said we might get together at Perino's, which, according to my Sources, was a favorite restaurant among conservative Republicans in Los Angeles—or at Chasen's, a favorite of movie people and conservative Republicans.

"You're living a little high on the hog," Haldeman said. "I used to go there when I had an expense account."

Anyhow, he thought Chasen's was closed for lunch on Saturdays, the day in question, but he would check it out or think of another good restaurant. Why didn't he pick me up at my hotel in his car? He would check out the restaurants and, in any event, come by about one o'clock. So much for my Sources, who didn't even know Chasen's was closed on Saturdays. I was trapped. Haldeman would choose the restaurant. He had already scored, dismissed my considered opinion, dictated change of turf. Round one to Haldeman.

Even worse, I had no idea where we would go, no way to leave word with a friend, with my agent or my attorney. I saw myself in the back seat of a limousine, between two goons, headed down a lonely road toward the beach, to a small Mexican restaurant serving enchiladas to CIA agents.

"I'll pick you up at your hotel, I'll be driving a blue T-Bird."

So that was to be it, a blue T-bird. A perfect undercover car. I was at his mercy.

In any case, that was my first exchange with Haldeman. It was not much—a few words only, neutral words, given in an even, pleasant voice, vigorous and warm, confident and attentive, healthy and slightly humorous, altogether the voice of a nice guy.

Three

JOE DiMaggio was in the coffee shop at the Beverly Wilshire Hotel. When I stepped through the door with my Friday morning papers, the cashier whispered to me, "Do you see who's here?"

"Who?"

"Joe DiMaggio."

"Where?"

"Over there, by the window."

I looked. There he was. Tanned, fit, healthy, wearing a sport shirt, open at the neck. His hair was gray; his eyes were clear. He looked good. He had a little paunch around the middle, but not much. I thought I remembered that DiMaggio always had that pear shape. Even in 1946, when he had just got back from the war, when he had hit twenty-five home runs, he had seemed thick around the middle. He had a small head, and he was thick around the middle.

Number five. I was pleased with myself, that I had remembered the number on DiMaggio's uniform.

"He looks good."

"Yeah, he looks great."

I sat down. The waitress came up to me. "Do you see who's here?"

"DiMaggio," I said.

"Yeah."

"Looks good," I said.

"Used to look better."

The waitress may have leered.

Everybody in the coffee shop was talking about Joe DiMaggio.

"Boy, you remember when Joe DiMaggio played for the Yankees? The world was a simpler place then."

"Who said that?"

Everyone said that.

The world always used to be simpler. If you were an old man in 1938, you thought the world was simpler when McKinley was President. And if you were Nan, watching from the window of the Drake Hotel while McKinley paraded down a Chicago street, you thought everything was simpler in the days of the Founding Fathers. And if you were Thomas Hutchinson, you thought life had never been so complicated as it was in 1773.

Those who find their own lives complicated, those who cannot imagine that life was ever complicated before they were born, often argue that democracy was a form of government well suited to the eighteenth century, when life was simpler, but that it is positively unworkable in the complex world of the twentieth century. Jeffersonian democracy was OK for an agrarian society, but in our new, postindustrial, computerized, interdependent, blah, blah, blah . . .

The new forms of government proposed in such conversations are never so new, either. The usual proposal—an oligarchy, with entry to its higher reaches based upon merit, dispensing centralized planning drafted by well-trained experts—appears to be more or less similar to the sort of government that gorillas have, a fact that does not argue forcefully for either the newness of oligarchy nor its inherent suitability for subtle and complex times and minds.

The sense that things must once have been simpler is, of course, called nostalgia. Nostalgia is a sensation so common, and so universally despised by grown-up realists, that it deserves some examination. Most human beings long to return to a time of comfort and security, to return in fact to their childhood homes. "Nostalgia" is derived from the Greek *nostos*, which means simply a "return home"—and most of us have schooled ourselves to despise such soft, sentimental feelings. Conceivably, some Darwinian imperative is at work here: We must despise nostalgia in order to go out in the world and contribute to the gross national product; yet, at the same time, nostalgia may be all that keeps worldlings from destroying their planet. If life is meaningless and futile, why not let the world go smash? Or, if the only point to earthly life is to get to heaven, why not let the world go smash? We may have no better, no more profound, reason for keeping the world intact than a simple-minded, nostalgic, absurd sentimental attachment.

Moreover, it is in the home of childhood that our understandings of such things as trust, fairness, getting our own way, and sharing are learned. So, too, no doubt, is love of home, of homeland, of country. These are not negligible matters that we shed as we grow into adult ways of thinking. These are the skeletons that inform—that, literally, give form from within—to our lives.

The childhood home that I remember was one in Palatine, Illinois, a suburb about thirty miles northwest of Chicago. The house was white, a large white house, with white pillars at the front door and, along one side, a large screened porch. It had green shutters at each of the windows, and it seemed to me vast, as vast as the white house in Washington, D.C., and it was surrounded by a great sloping lawn and huge trees on one side of the house that thickened into woods in back of the house. Steps led down to the open lawn, to a birdbath and space for games of touch football, and places to stand to have snapshots taken on Saturdays and Sundays.

As I look back at the pictures in the photograph album, I see a little boy, who looks astonishingly like my own son (is it, after all, all genetics?) smiling and laughing and throwing baseballs, dressed in sailor suits and in white shoes that lace high up on the ankles, swaggering, toting a gun, wearing my father's hat, grinning, chortling, giggling, screaming with laughter, trying to swing a tennis racket. My memory accords with these pictures of my childhood. I had a wonderful time, and I saw no reason that happiness should ever end.

Like most all memoirists, I make the house of my childhood sound larger and grander than it can have been, for we were, as I said, a middle-class family, a bourgeois family, not a family of extraordinary wealth. And although I was always jealous of the rich, and of their sense of ease, their assumption of owning any space they walk into, their worldliness, their good looks and accents and familiarity with French—and, thus, to compensate myself late in life, I spruce up the home of my childhood—still, it does seem to me that I grew up in a comparative bastion of wealth and privilege, comfort, security, tennis rackets, footballs, tricycles, and sleds.

I do see, though, that sometime in 1943, sometime when I was five years old, an inexplicable sense of uncertainty enters these snapshots. That, too, is like the pictures of my own son. I am at a loss to explain this uneasy feeling. My father, who worked then for the Commonwealth Edison Company of Chicago, was transferred often in those years from town to town, and perhaps that explains it somewhat. Perhaps I was torn away from my friends too often, torn away from that wonderful white mansion in Palatine. My father was young, and ambitious, and doubtless subject to the anxieties I had as a young father, unsure I would be able to make my way, support my family. And was my mother, too, unsure about what she had taken on with her three children? I was the youngest of three, the only boy, and now, as I look through the album for pictures of myself, I notice my mother, and she looks tired, very tired and worn and sometimes sad.

Were they concerned about the war, and too concerned, perhaps, with getting on in the world? Had my father's father, refugee from Manchester and, long ago, from famine, burdened this young man with too many worries about working hard and behaving well and getting on? God, how tired my mother looks, standing out on that lovely lawn in Palatine, a pretty, slender young woman, too young and lively to be so soon burdened by a household, and my father well turned out in his three-piece white summer suit with well-pressed trousers (pressed just that morning by my mother?), and me, standing handsomely in my white summer shorts, concentrating on something I held in my hands. Pulling the wings off a butterfly, perhaps.

Then, in 1945, after the war, in a new town then, in Streator, Illinois, farther south, I see us all cheered up, and there is my mother at a horse show with Rosemary Mulvihill, her friend, an older woman, and my mother is laughing and looks strong and vibrant again. And there is my father, looking far more established, more confident, more middle-aged, more my age. He has put on a little weight, and it looks as though he has learned a thing or two—about business no doubt, about the world, perhaps even about his wife and children.

And there am I, with a dog, my new dog, my Irish Setter Pat, holding him, hugging him, and there is my friend Scott with his funny knit cap, black and yellow, and that painful way he had, that hurts me still, of hunching his shoulders up so tightly because he was so unsure, and there is the pup tent in which we camped out, and the old tan African explorer's hat —what are they called?—that I used to have, and Scott's sister—oh, how beautiful she is still in that snapshot, beautiful, blonde, and silken—the two of us sitting together in the black leather horse carriage with the white spoke wheels—and thus we had come through those years, whatever ghosts had caused their anxiety, as I know my own son will, too.

For quite a long time, I thought I wanted to be a girl. The women in my family, as far as I could see, were altogether the most appealing kind of people. I have two sisters, one just a couple of years older than I, and another a couple of years older still. Both of them look now just as they have always looked: The elder is pretty and bright-eyed, eager, lively, with a natural talent for drawing and painting and designing. My younger sister is pretty, too, pretty and blonde and, then as now, squishy and literary.

My mother seemed always to know precisely how I felt about everything and, indeed, to be able to feel it, too. She understood everything without words. She understood politics and philosophy and theology, all without a need to express anything except with a look or a smile or a light kiss on the forehead. Even still today, when I discuss some tortuous problem with my mother, whether about my own life or some problem of the world's, she need say only "yes" or "I know" with a slight inclination of the head, a certain intonation, an inflection, a look, and I know she has understood the problem—not abstractly, never abstractly, never in cool philosophical terms, not in the reasoned syllogisms of a rational system of thought, but with a recognition of the subtleties and nuances and warm complexities and contradictions of the human condition.

My mother and her mother, Nan, shared this profound and sophisticated sense of life. Their way of perceiving is often called intuitive, but that seems to me a shallow, superficial thing compared to their genius for complex means of thought-feeling. In my mother and my grandmother seemed an inexhaustible source of good, secure, and vaulting human possibility, of freedom and love, of contentment and excitement.

For a good long time, I thought that all that this meant was that I wanted to be a girl. For a good long time, it seemed to me that to be a girl meant to be kind and light-spirited, to be flexible, perceptive, warm, to be home, to be free, to be creative, to be inventive with paints and paper and yarn and needles and thread, to know stories about Indians and to play games of intricate dramaturgical imagination with paper dolls.

One fresh summer morning when I was three, or perhaps as old as four, I wandered out onto the porch where my sister, the squishy one, was getting out her paper dolls. She had a large collection of paper dolls, and I was greatly impressed by the neatness and precision with which she had cut out their clothes. When I was three or four years old, I arrived at the conclusion that girls are neat and boys are messy. I have not been able to change her mind about this childish perception or countless, unknown, others. I knelt down on the porch next to my sister, on a woven straw mat that covered the porch floor and scratched my bare knees. I watched her take the paper dolls out of the box, thinking as I watched her that she knew, and I knew, that I would never be able to put the paper dolls back into the box as neatly as she had. I thought that she might ask me if I would like to play with her.

No one else was around. As far as I knew, she was not expecting a friend to join her.

"Can I play with you?"

My sister almost sneered: "Boys don't play with paper dolls."

Her reply made me dizzy. I nearly reeled from the shock of it. Had I not played paper dolls with her before? She could hardly deny it. She certainly remembered how angry she had been at me for botching up some of the clothes when I had tried to cut them out, how she had criticized me for my sloppy, imprecise coloring job. No. There could be no doubt of this. I had, upon occasion, played paper dolls with my sister. I could get witnesses if need be.

Still, her reply had been definitive. There was no hope of appeal, I could tell from her tone of voice. I wandered—weaving from side to side, it seemed, light-headed, on the verge of fainting perhaps, the landscape whiting out into a sickening glare around the edges—out the door, down the steps, into the yard, lost, alone, abandoned, disoriented. Then, around the corner of the house came a girl my sister's age. She asked if my sister was at home, and I told her to look on the porch. This girl, I noticed, was carrying a box of paper dolls.

Thus I was cut off from the female members of my family—or, if not cut off from them, separated from them, shunted over to my father's side of the household, to the side of businessmen, business suits, rep stripe ties—and those other things I hate as—what?

Symbols of my father? Or symbols of the things that took my father from me and away into his office?

I missed my father terribly as a child. He was away much of the time, having to travel—as an area manager in the early years of my childhood—from town to town to oversee the operations of his electric company, while I was learning to fend for myself in a house full of women. When snowstorms swept across the Middle West, with ice and wind that blasted across the plains, piling drifts against our house, making icicles two and three feet long, then the electrical wires would whip and sway and crack apart and fall to the ground, and the lights would go out, and my father would be off for the night to make sure the work crews repaired the lines properly. He would drive the icy roads through the night, and I imagined him out there, in danger, battling the winds and the cold and bringing light and warmth back to the world.

I missed him, and, when he returned, I feared him. I thought for a long time that I feared the grown-up man of him, and no doubt I did fear him just for being the powerful figure he was, for being hearty and strong and, while not overbearing, often booming in his voice. But I enjoyed all of that, too, and I enjoyed the life of a boy, of playing catch with my father, of showing him how fast I could run, of feeling his strength when he caught me and showing him mine in return. I enjoyed going for drives with my father, and talking to him and enjoying his knowledge of the world, his command of facts and data, the force of his reason—and yet, from time to time, I would remember the fear.

One night when Nan was putting me to bed, I asked her if she believed in God.

"Yes, of course."

"Do you believe in heaven?"

"Yes, certainly."

Then came the big question: "Do you believe in hell?"

With a smile: "No."

I was thunderstruck, and distrustful, and, amid it all, I noticed she had smiled. Hell did not even scare her the littlest bit. It was clear she thought the idea was almost laughable, almost contemptible. But I could not, even so, quite trust her. I tried out my Jesuitical reasoning.

"How can you believe in heaven and not believe in hell?"

"Because God is good. He wouldn't punish people forever just for making mistakes."

Erasmus had not been more profound than my grandmother, and she relieved my mind tremendously, though, of course, at the same time, she gave me another burden. I was presented with a dilemma: My father, a devout Catholic, believed in hell. There was the crux of the matter: My mother and grandmother were Protestant—not even quite Protestant, really, but only, vaguely, "Christian." My father was Catholic. To side with the women in my family was to make me—what?—a girl? Impossible. Someone at least who shrank from the hard facts of the world? Nonetheless, to side with my father was to make me—no doubt of it, for I was a bad boy with bad thoughts and bad wishes—destined to go straight to hell, straight as an arrow to eternal damnation, to fire and brimstone, and writhing, naked, bleeding, burning bodies, squirming in cauldrons of shit and snot.

It was a dilemma that required a sly, delicate Zen escape act; each apparent path to freedom led to other traps, to other dilemmas, to other binds and boxes. I was properly caught, and I writhed and squirmed, and, just to keep my spirits up, I found myself a scapegoat. I blamed all my problems on my father's mother, the German from the good St. Louis family, Bertha—or, as we called her, Mee Mom—and I hated her with a violent passion.

It is bad enough to be a German Protestant. It is bad enough to be a Catholic. But what is absolutely fierce is to be a German Protestant who converts to Catholicism. That was Mee Mom. She had rebelled against her self-esteeming German Protestant family, married a lowborn Catholic, and then—out of love for her new husband? out of duty? out of rebellious hatred for her parents?—she had set about winning the competition for the best Catholic of the New World. She won.

When Mee Mom came to visit in my childhood home, she was always dressed and ready for church on Sundays a good half hour or forty-five minutes ahead of everyone else, and, while the rest of us mortally

CHARLES L. MEE, JR.

sinful slothful children scurried to get ready for church, she would be sitting quietly downstairs, lips firmly pursed, precious old prayer book in her white gloved hand, waiting—a thunderously silent reprimand of her grandchildren, and of her son who sired that sinful undisciplined brood—so loose and unorganized, so catch-as-catch-can, so—how do you say?—so American! As Nan believed in heaven, so Bertha believed in hell.

I had a clear and vibrant vision of her face that I carried about in my imagination at all times; it was a prunish face, screwed up in constant disapproval and distaste, a face that thought it smelled something unpleasant, a face that suspected me of backsliding and laxity, of laziness and sinfulness and thoughts of sex and other dirty things, a face that said that I was a nasty, sinful little boy who would be most uncommonly fortunate to escape eternal damnation and that I must, in any case, not presume and not be naughty, consider myself lucky for what I had, thank God for it and be grateful to my parents and country and ask for nothing more, since anything more would be too much; she had a face that said I ought not aspire too high, a face that said be humble, a face that said be modest, beware of pride, be nice, be good, hold yourself back or God will strike you down, say your prayers, do your duty, seek mortification, avoid pleasure, and thank God nightly for all your many blessings.

I could afford to hate Mee Mom, since she was not often around, coming only occasionally for visits, and so I had no chance to grow to know her and so diffuse and confuse the hatred I had contrived to harbor for her, but she was, certainly, a sitting duck for hatred, with her strict German ways and her passionate ambition, which I could not understand, to achieve holiness.

Both of her sons, my father and his brother, Bill, became businessmen and so escaped the intensity of Mee Mom's religious devotion. One of her daughters, my Aunt Madge, became the mother of one nun and two priests. My cousin Charlie escaped a religious vocation, but he had to be wonderfully clever to do it. Charlie was as bright as the other children in the family, probably not brighter, but perhaps shrewder. He developed a talent as a physicist, a remarkable talent as a physicist: He not only understood Einstein's theory of relativity, but also added a corollary to it. Because of this, the family concluded that he ought to be allowed to pursue physics, since God evidently meant him to do so.

I always liked Charlie, for escaping Mee Mom and Aunt Madge in the first instance, and for showing me how to fix a phonograph scientifically in the second instance. He came to visit for the Christmas holidays one year when he was in college. The "reject" button on our phonograph did not work properly, and so, as a favor to my father, Charlie took the phonograph apart while I watched and then, very scientifically, played it over and over and over again each step of the way of disassembling so that he would know just how to put it together again. We got it apart in one day and continued to work on it for the full fourteen days of his vacation, trying to get it back together again. Still today there are three pieces in a box in a drawer somewhere. We could not find where to put them. The local repairmen could not even recognize the three extra pieces, nor find any place in the phonograph where any piece seemed to be missing. The whole thing seemed to have been put back together again perfectly, only it didn't work. No one was ever able to figure it out. Charlie is now a very distinguished radio astronomer: He spends all his time listening to the universe. I don't believe he is coming to any conclusions. He is just listening. He has not started to take anything apart.

Mee Mom's only other daughter, my father's other sister, became a nun: Sister Lucy. She was a whirl-wind. She was the head of an order of nuns that had its national or international or whatever headquarters in Wisconsin, and she passed through my hometown once in a while. She would fling herself off the train while it was still moving and come crashing and flapping down onto the platform like a giant bird, like a pterodactyl, and she always smelled faintly of brisk-ness and Easter flower. She swooped and leaped and pounced, and she talked continuously, eagerly, ener-getically, forcefully, and then, all of a sudden, she was back on the train, swoop, swoop, and away, hugs, blessings, a small parting God homily, and up, flapping, onto the train and off, down the track and on to Wisconsin.

I thought she was insufferably self-involved and impressed with herself, but I never dared let myself think such thoughts for too long, since she was a nun and consequently holy. I felt little in the way of affection for her; I knew she felt none or little for me. I was one of God's little creatures to her, precious for that reason, if for any at all. I hated her a little bit, but not much; I knew I did not understand her, and I did not usually bother to think of her at all. I don't think she bothered to think of me. I don't recall hearing from her at all.

Several years ago, I received a letter from her. I was inordinately pleased to see Sister Lucy's return address on the envelope. By this time I had long since left the Church and felt free of old emotional turmoil about it. I was happy to hear from my aunt the nun, who was so brisk and of whom, after all, I discovered I had some fond feelings and some lurking admiration. In her letter she wrote to say that she was dying, dying of cancer, and had not much longer to live. She wished to beg my forgiveness—and I could not imagine why. She had harbored ill feelings for me all these years, she said; she had not spoken to me all these years. My God, I thought, I hadn't noticed: Here she has been bearing me a grudge for some reason, bearing the burden herself of that grudge, and I had not even noticed; I had not expected to hear from her ever, and so I could hardly have missed hearing from her.

She had not spoken to me, she said, because she had not been able in her heart to accept my marriage. My marriage! So that was it: because I had divorced Claire Lu and married Suzi. She had not been able to get over that divorce! How sad. She had been, Sister Lucy said, as she now realized, perhaps too rigid (I stuck at that "perhaps"; I stopped there and had to work up my will again to continue reading) and too narrow in her view of things. She realized now (now! now, after a whole ecumenical movement and Vatican councils and God knows what-all it had taken her, unable to come to any fair-minded judgment of her own, dependent upon the dictates of an antediluvian pope!) that times had changed and perhaps she should have been more accepting of my marriage. Could I please forgive her for this transgression so that she could go peacefully to her God, and would I please accept her loving affection in Christ.

Would I, would I, would I, so that she, bless her selfish black heart, could go peacefully to her God, would I forgive her implacable, hateful, bilious grudge. The gorge rose up to choke me. I was not, it turned out, as free of Church and guilt and antique rage as I had complimented myself for being. How could she, the head of a religious order, be so inconceivably un-Christian as she had been? No, I would not forgive her. No, I would not. It would not be that easy, for I had been tormented by this sort of damned, grudge-filled, hate-filled, harsh, black, unloving Christianity for too many years. No. Let Sister Lucy feel the tortures of her religion. Let her fry in hell.

And yet, how could I be so enraged? I had not suffered from her grudge. I had not even known of it. It was absurd. I was above it. I had long ago outlived these vengeful emotions. Of course I would forgive her. Not that it mattered. Not that she needed forgiveness. It was all too quaint. I picked up pen and paper and wrote, expressing my regrets about her sickness, sending her some human warmth, some love, some acceptance, and accepting her apologies—adding that, of course, apologies were hardly necessary; I had not noticed she had not been speaking to me. Who would have noticed? Who cared? Who gave a damn what she thought?

I tore up this letter and tried again with expressions of regret and love and acceptance. I tried six or eight times. But I could not do it. Each time the gorge rose up, and I lashed out at her, or added something cutting, something snide, something mean, something biting, some phrase with a double entendre. She died before I was able to frame a letter of some few, simple sentences.

I see now, as I never saw before, what a vast and definitive break my father made from the fears and rages of his own times, to what an enormous extent he broke free, with his moustache and his cocktail parties and his children who became neither priests nor nuns. If Nan is right, if there is a heaven, surely my father will go there.

Our own time is full of itself, full of its presumed complexities, full of the momentousness of the changes that are occurring around us, of new freedoms, of the end of the traditional family and sexual roles, of the breakdown of such institutions as churches, of future shock, of the ever-accelerating rate of the rate of change. Yes, it may be so, it may be. But, my father was born of immigrants who changed their entire ways of life; he was born into a Victorian family and speaks with a generation that lives in communes; he has lived through world wars, through a time of seeing the whole nature of warfare change, from his father teaching fencing in the Coldstream Guards to mass democratic wars, to guerrilla wars and the possibility of suitcase nuclear wars; he has witnessed awesome changes in beliefs in the nature of God, of the human species, of growth and progress, of the physical universe, of biology—you name it. In my father's lifetime, everything has changed. It is not possible that in my own lifetime more than everything will change.

And yet, astonishingly, civilization did not come to an end during my father's lifetime. For all the change, for all the disintegration and reformulation of ideas and institutions and flotsam and whatnot, the world did not come to an end. It may be that all our new turmoil will not finish off civilization either. It may even be that what we are now feeling is a vast slowing down of civilization, a time of consolidation, of rest, of respite, a time of quiescence while the last traces of the old "modern" civilization that began with the Renaissance gently settle beneath the surface of the sea, Atlantis-like, leaving us with a new age, in which we are all, already, without even realizing it, quite at home.

But let me look again on the face of my grandmother Mee Mom. She stands in the backyard of my home in Barrington, the place that still is home to me, that has been home since I was ten years old. She stands in front of the flowering lilac bush. She is wearing her sturdy, sensible black shoes and her silk print dress with its worried little design in black and white and black and white and black and white. Her fine white hair is just so in place, and her glasses with the fine, slender silver rims reminiscent of those her husband wore those years ago before he died, when was it then?, when I was eight or maybe nine, just a year or two or three before. She stands there, and my arm is around her shoulder, awkwardly, dutifully clutching her upper arm, just at her triceps. And there, more surprisingly, her arm is around my waist, but casually so and comfortably so, and with apparent affection. And she is smiling. She is smiling happily, easily, brilliantly, joyfully. There is not a trace of stern disapproval on her face. It may even be she rather liked me. I wonder if she sensed how I hated her. I wonder if it hurt her feelings. I hope not. She was quite a woman. Formidable.

She can afford to smile, for whatever guilt she ever felt for any reason she accepted, and confessed, and practiced atonement, But I, I would have none of that, I would accept no guilt, wear no mourning for anything, for original sin or the death of Christ or any of the other death-loving rites of the Catholic Church. No, I accepted none of it for years; for years I stayed ahead of it; but in the end it catches up with us and wears us down, and, in the end, we must accept it, in whatever guise.

Among the magazines I took with me into the coffee shop at the Beverly Wilshire was a copy of *Harper's* magazine, which contained an article by Peter Marin on "The New Narcissism," in which he said: "We take coffee and sugar in the mornings, and even that simple act immerses us immediately in the larger world. Both the sugar and coffee have come from specific places, have been harvested by specific persons, most probably in a country where the land belongs by right to others than those who hold it, where the wages paid those who work are exploitive and low. No doubt, too, the political system underlying the distribution of land is maintained in large part by the policies enacted and the armies acting in our name— and the reason we enjoy the coffee while others harvest it has nothing to do with individual will and everything to do with economics and history.

"That, I believe, is what each of us already knows —no matter how much we pretend we do not. Our lives are crowded with the presence of unacknowledged others, upon whom our well-being and privilege depend. The shadows of those neglected others—

dying in Asia, hungry in Africa, impoverished in our country—fall upon every one of our private acts, darken the household and marriage bed for each of us. We try to turn away, but even the desperate nature of our turning is a function of their unacknowledged presence, and they are with us even in the vehemence with which we pretend they are not. Something in each of us . . . aches with their presence, aches for the world, for why else would we be in so much pain?"

And so in the end I am caught, and in the end, I, too, say with my grandmother, standing in her dress of black and white and black and white, that I believe in the seven Corporal Works of Mercy: to feed the hungry, to give drink to the thirsty, to clothe the naked, to shelter the homeless, to visit the sick and prisoners, to ransom captives, and to bury the dead— and even in the seven Spiritual Works of Mercy: to teach the ignorant, to counsel the doubtful, to console the sad, to reprove the sinner, to forgive the offender, to bear with the oppressive and troublesome, and to pray for us all. I can no longer take pleasure and solace in the pageantry of the Church, especially now that its liturgy has been rendered into barbarous English; I cannot any longer quite connect with all of the richness of the vestments, the thick sweetness of the incense, the hazy mysteries of the Gregorian chant, even though I miss them all sometimes; I can no longer bear the chop logic of the theology, the narrowness and meanness of the ministers of God, the fear, the terror of the nuns. But I do believe in the works of mercy. So, let us now exchange letters of forgiveness, and let there be peace.

I remember much of my Catholic childhood; I feel that, like facing the prospect of hanging, it wonderfully concentrated the mind. I faced hell each day that I awoke: I say it now without rancor or special sense of melodrama, I say quite simply that every day I had a catechism lesson first thing in the morning. Whether one did or did not learn the answers to the questions in the Baltimore catechism—learn them precisely correctly, to the very jot and title, as I understood it—determined whether or not one would go to hell for all eternity.

It is not possible to live under such pressure as this indefinitely, and so I, and all my school friends, learned various ways of coping. Some dropped out of the Church completely at the age of seven or eight, saying, in effect, they did not believe in any of the teachings of the nuns for one moment; they knew perfectly well they were not going to hell, and they fully intended to be disobedient, use filthy language, and have fun. I thought them remarkably brave, and foolhardy; I knew for certain that they would be extremely lucky, unusually extremely lucky, to escape damnation. Some of them, the really foul ones, fascinated me especially: I looked at them as future inhabitants of hell, and I thought they were very curious, repellent specimens, intriguing in the way that cockroaches are.

Others of my school chums sold out at once, announced their intentions of becoming nuns or priests, signed up to serve as altar boys, and prayed their neurons out. They were accepted by the nuns as members of the Elect and so, strangely, were relieved of their fears to a large extent: As long as they stayed intended priests and nuns they were safe. These children were easy to pick out. I knew that Tom Tobin and Bob Fedota would become priests. And they did.

Most of the rest of us learned politics. We squirmed and wheedled; we dealt and bargained; we lied and cheated; we presented false fronts and secretly prayed with genuine fervor; we learned to sneak, to manipulate, to smile, to lurk, we learned how to manage things, how to keep things in balance, how to be good administrators, businessmen, bookkeepers (two sets, double entry), how to rig things, how to schmooze, how to slip, skirt, slide by, get around, and look entirely guileless; we knew how to seem sincere, self-righteous, innocent, outraged, straightforward, unpretentious, and idealistic.

These are the politics of a totalitarian country, which the Catholic Church certainly was; and I have always felt that I understood the principles of democracy with a special keenness because I grew up under totalitarianism.

To call the Catholic Church totalitarian is not to denigrate it. The Church knows what it is and is satisfied with itself. The Church aspires, in the name of helping its members to eternal salvation, to control not only the behavior but also words and thoughts of

Catholics. "Bless me, Father, I confess that I have sinned in thought, word, and deed" is how the Catholic confession begins. People do not merely go to jail for committing antisocial acts; people go to hell for thinking evil thoughts. The Catholic Church was in the business of thought control long before Joseph Stalin was born—and has always been more successful at it than the Russians have ever been.

I hope the Church will not take these remarks amiss. I doubt that it will. The Church knows what it is doing, and it believes it is justified. It believes that it serves such a high goal that these lowly means are entirely justified. Most totalitarian states—though their goals are less exalted than eternal salvation of the souls of men and women—believe that the end justifies the means, too. And it may be true that if one believes life has a purpose beyond living that the end does justify the means. In a democracy—which allows people to believe that life is the end, or that people should be free to pursue whatever end they wish—we must believe that the means *are* the end.

In any case, by the time I was in eighth grade at St. Anne's School, I think it is true—such was the excellence of the educational system I had been through —that I was ready to graduate. I know that I was ready; in retrospect, I can reconstruct what seems to me now to have been my final examinations. I helped to write and edit and assemble the customary yearbook for the eighth-grade graduating class. My mother saved this yearbook for me all of these years; I wonder if she knew at the time just how interesting it might be to me one day.

Among the photographs in this book is a set that records the celebrations of Confirmation Day. Its meaning was described in a passage written for the yearbook by Johnnie Goodwillie: "Confirmation is the sacrament through which we receive the Holy Ghost to make us soldiers of Jesus Christ ready to profess our Faith both in word and in action." Right above Johnnie Goodwillie's words is a Confirmation Day picture of Charlie Wisner.

To memorialize his own confirmation, Charlie chose to stand next to a bookcase to have his picture taken. On top of the bookcase was a vase of flowers and a statue of the Virgin Mary. Charlie wore the standard confirmation robes. He placed one hand atop the bookcase, and—here's the touch of genius—he placed the other hand, with a violent cynicism, over his heart. Snap. Click.

Charlie was admired and feared for this bold act of his. It was obvious to all of his peers that his pose was so cynical as to be positively sacrilegious. The great game was always to skirt the edge of mockery— but never to cross it; if the nuns ever realized they were being mocked, their rage was awful. The children waited for Sister Amelberga to fall wrathfully upon Charlie. As it turned out, Sister Amelberga loved the picture.

One learns a special way of talking in a totalitarian country, too. Each graduating class at St. Anne's chose

CHARLES L. MEE, JR.

a class motto. Here is Claire Bick, the class president, on the motto for her class: "One bright morning we sat in our classroom discussing what our motto should be for our last school year at St. Anne's. After a short time of pondering over the different mottoes, we finally selected this one: Build for Eternity, not for Fame. This had been proposed to us [by Sister Amelberga, as Claire delicately refrained from saying, and so made it appear a result of divine inspiration], and like a magic word, the echo of this motto resounded in every heart, and unanimously it was chosen, not only as the motto of our last school year, but for our entire life."

Claire could have stopped here in her account of the class motto, but she was as furious as her classmates at having this homily jammed down her throat in the expectation that she should be grateful for having been used. So Claire went on, making a few more passes with her trowel: "How many times during this year did we not feel discouraged and disheartened at our little failures, but one thought braced us up: 'No matter if I failed—I worked for God's honor, and by Him I did not fail for eternity, although I was not successful here in this vale of tears.'"

It seemed to me that Claire might have been somewhat less fulsome; but this sort of piety knows no bounds, and, in time, like good Pavlovians, many of the children come to believe their own poses, or come, more confusingly, to mix sincerity, hypocrisy, guilt, shame, hope, love, and terror into passages like this one, which I wrote myself, and which sounds, in retrospect, like a confession at a Stalinist show trial:

"We, the pupils of the eighth grade, devote this page to dear Sister Amelberga . . . to you, Sister, our true friend, to whom we owe so much, we shall never be able to compensate as we should. However, we shall remember you in the mass—the mass that you tried to teach us to love. To you, a sacrificing sister, we owe much for your untiring zeal and interest in our religious and academic education.

"Your incessant words of encouragement, with that constant reminder of frequently making a good intention to merit a reward for eternity, and of remaining near to our Lord and His Blessed Mother, with the many sacrifices you made for our happiness, we wish to extend our sincere thanks.

"Your daily emphasis on obedience to those in authority and a sacrificing spirit for others will be a beacon light for us in our tasks of everyday life."

When I wrote that, I meant it, and I meant it very deeply and passionately and sincerely. I meant it with my whole heart and my whole soul. I understand that Cardinal Mindszenty, in the end, came to love his captors, too.

To live in a totalitarian state, if you live at all, if you are not liquidated or expelled, you must, in order to survive, *be* someone else. You cannot be yourself. You must commit a willing act of self-annihilation. That is to say, it is not at all possible to live in a totalitarian state. You must die one way or another.

And that is why people who have lived in totalitarian states don't like them.

Sister Amelberga was hardly Stalin. She was probably as decent a person as most. She was, I like to think, enmeshed in a system that she loved and needed and did not understand, and she was fated, as characters in Greek tragedies are fated, to play out her role. In playing out her role, she had a pervasive influence, as her sister Sisters did, through eight years of Catholic schooling, on me.

The nuns produced a child who tended to be highly moralistic, keenly attuned to the practice of hyprocrisy in himself and others, a great practitioner of hypocrisy, a child (and man) who could lapse into sincerity and piety at the drop of a holy medal, a child respectful and fearful of authority. He became uncommonly adept at pleasing his teachers—and he detested himself for it. He was teacher's pet, the top student in his class, an altar boy. He genuinely wished to be a good boy, and the harder he tried, the more he succeeded, the phonier he knew he was. And yet he still wanted to be a good boy, and he had a great, heaven-or-hell need to think himself good. He would never rid himself of this maddening, indoctrinated need. In the end, the child bolted from the Church, in part because he could not bear to have the Church keep reminding him what an evil person he was. Given a choice between self-hatred (personal death, suicide) and flight, he fled.

He had been raised according to a set of rules of

behavior and thought control that had not changed much since they had been set down by a monk in the ninth century. In many ways, he felt that he had, himself, been raised in the ninth century. For those who find this notion incredible or exaggerated or somewhat absurd, let me quote some of the medieval rules of daily life as set down by St. Benedict:

Not to embrace pleasures.

To become a stranger to the doings of the world.

To suffer persecution for justice's sake.

Not to be proud.

To attribute what one finds good in oneself to God, not to oneself.

To recognize, on the other hand, that evil is done by us, and we should impute it to ourselves.

To long for eternal life with all spiritual desire.

Not to give in to the desires of the flesh.

To hate one's own will.

Not to love frequent and loud laughter.

To obey the commands of the abbot in all things.

To recognize that God knows all things in all places.

To fear the day of judgment.

To be terrified of hell.

To keep the vision of death daily before one's eyes.

I arrived in the twentieth century amazed and delighted. My pleasure was even more intense than that of a refugee from Eastern Europe. I came to a free country—only to discover that its natives took their liberties so much for granted that they were neglecting and losing them. Having always had freedom, they did not know what they had, much less how to keep it. They did not even know how to think about it, any more than fish know how to think about water.

In any case, just as I was leaving the Catholic Church, it seemed to me that my country was stumbling into it. Just as I came running lickety-split out of the Catholic Church with a vivid fear of totalitarianism and of any threats to individual liberty and autonomy, with fear of all those who might be trying to keep track of my private thoughts by way of bugging or confession, just as I was moving into newfound freedom, it seemed to me that my country was moving—without knowing it—into the sort of hypocrisy, bureaucracy, rituals of royalism, backstage political bossism, conscious manipulation of thought and feeling, appeals to absolute good and evil, references to eternal salvation (or national security), techniques of inducing anxiety and fears of being unconventional, requirements of steely discipline against an implacable common foe, the need for massive retaliation against the Devil, a sacrificial tithing for the common defense, the centralization of political power and authority and administration, characteristic of the totalitarian Roman Catholic Church—and all this without even promising to get me to heaven.

George Washington advised his descendants to avoid foreign entanglements because he understood, as we seem to have forgotten, that any nation that is too active in foreign affairs will find it exceedingly difficult to remain a democratic country. America's central government was charged by the Founding Fathers with providing for the common defense, and, indeed, the common defense is really the singular need for a central government. If there is no external enemy, then there is no need for a government to take care of and protect the people. An external enemy creates a potent need for government. If a government has none, it will often make one up—or make a monster of one who is merely bad, or go out searching for trouble instead of simply defending against it, or exacerbating differences instead of mollifying them. Such tricks are as old as the usages of the old European monarchy—or older, as old as the Catholic Church and the Devil. If there is no Devil, if there is no threat of hell, then there's very little need for the Catholic Church.

From this, much else follows: The central government was not built up as a result of Roosevelt's New Deal, not at all. Keynesian economics were not given lavish attention during the 1930s. On the contrary: In 1939, after a decade of depression, after the Civilian Conservation Corps, the Public Works Administration, the Civil Works Administration, the Works Progress Administration, the Agricultural Adjustment Act, the Social Security Act, and all the rest of the New Deal efforts on behalf of social justice, the federal budget was $9 billion. After America entered

World War II, in 1945, it was $100 billion. War ran up the budget; war ran up the Keynesian deficit; war made the big federal government; war concentrated power in the hands of the executive, and war—Cold War—continued to do those same things after 1945 as before.

The central government was built up by Truman and by Eisenhower, by Kennedy and by Johnson and by Nixon and by Ford. It was a truly bipartisan effort —which is to say that both parties agreed not to debate the one issue, the common defense, on which the need for the federal government is founded, from which all its other powers derive, and that involves the most important question, peace or war, that confronts any government. The fruition of this bipartisan effort was to add agency after agency for the management first of defense, then of defense readiness, then of business, then of agriculture, then of the very bits and pieces of daily life, so that by now our daily lives, our common welfare, our old New Deal, have all been altogether suffocated by our new religion.

Have things really become more complicated in our time? Perhaps our age is not so complex after all; perhaps, instead, we have simplified life too extremely in these past few decades, reducing it simplemindedly to the disciplines of money and power, trying to purge our lives of contradictions and anxieties and complications, trying to purge our Republic of the bothersome, messy, complex demands of democracy and to transform it into some brutish simpleminded tyranny of the rich and the strong. Perhaps we need to go back to the complications and messes and nuances of Joe DiMaggio's era. We have got, I think, to a point of deadliness. Life is more various and subtler than we have come to allow; the world is more complicated, politicians (and people) more devious than we admitted to ourselves for a while. We've simplified our lives and our perceptions and our politics and our public world too fatally much; it is the simplification of churches and popes and kings and despots, of those who deal with purposes beyond life. We must deal with life; and we must revive our democratic usages to do so—for only democracy can deal with life, where the means *are* the end.

I must have been speaking out loud, because the man next to me in the Beverly Wilshire coffee shop was speaking, evidently in response to something I had said. He was a man in his middle fifties, I would guess, conservatively dressed in a pinstripe blue suit with a silk paisley tie. We did not introduce ourselves to one another, but I noticed that he was having English muffins with orange marmalade, and so let me call him the muffin man.

MUFFIN MAN: Fuck it, that's what I say. Fuck it. To hell with it. Fuck it. I don't give a shit. Look, I don't know anything about Stalin, but I figure we made a monster out of him. We made this huge god-damned monster out of Stalin. Then, in order to fight him, we made a monster out of ourselves. Two great big monsters grappling all over the world. So sure, that's right. We made a monster. America's a monster.

MEE: Yeah?

MUFFIN MAN: Of course it is. Sure it is. It's a goddamned monster.

MEE: How do you know you're not projecting your own private visions of monsters onto the . . . .

MUFFIN MAN: What kind of screwball Chinese box question is that? I say we made a monster. That's all. A fucking fire-breathing monster.

MEE: So what are you going to . . . .

MUFFIN MAN: Smash it. Kill it. What the hell. That's what's happening, anyway. That's what two hundred million people are doing anyway. Two hundred million people are gradually withdrawing their support for the monster. You don't really have to rise up and kill the monster. All you have to do is stop giving it food. Stop feeding the monster and it will die. That's all. Just let it die. That's what two hundred million people are doing anyway, bless their hearts. The middle class no longer believes this government or trusts this government. The middle class is withdrawing. To hell with the Hippies. Screw the Hippies. The Hippies didn't do a damned thing. But the middle class has finally given up on this government and that means it's gonna die, it's gonna smash. It's gonna starve to death. You can't continue running a goverment when nobody trusts it. The politicians keep saying, why don't people trust the government?

What's this crazy irrational thing they have of distrusting the government? But it's not trustworthy, that's why they don't trust it.

MEE: But you can't let the government go smash. You can't live in a world without a government.

MUFFIN MAN: Look, what is this thing you have about the government? What is this emotional lack in your life that the government is filling for you? What the hell's the matter with you? I mean, I don't know. Either you're fulfilling some cuckoo screwball bullshit need in your life with all this involvement with politics, or else you're just caught up in the inflated stuff you expect from the government because you were raised under Roosevelt. You're used to being dependent on the government—for all of your emotional needs. Look, you gotta get over it. You've gotta learn to live without it. Look, for God's sakes, the government isn't really even very important. I mean, you know, it's not much more important than the Red Sox, finally.

MEE: Well, except that the Red Sox don't kill people.

MUFFIN MAN: Look, right, OK, sure. Yeah. I see I'm going to have to cast this in some airtight form for you, right? Governments, it is true, have enormous powers to do evil. Governments do not, however, appear to have very much capacity to do good. So now, I ask you, what do you conclude from this? If this is the nature of government, the very best thing that could happen to governments is that they should absolutely disappear. If all they really do well is evil, let them disappear. We should be better off without them. Look, mainly people cope with the important things for themselves anyway. Mainly the things that matter in your life and mine are the things that you and I cope with ourselves, and politics can't do very much for the main stuff that we have in our lives.

MEE: They can do something for the . . .

MUFFIN MAN: The poor? Fuck the poor. Look—all you need to do for the poor is send them some money. That's all you need to do. All we're doing now with the government is sending money to the bureaucracy, not to the poor. Let the bureaucracy disappear. Let some checks be issued automatically to everyone who has a birth certificate. What do you think, they'll stop working when they have the money they need? Horse-shit. Everybody in this country works for more. More, more, more. That's all anybody wants. It is human nature not to want what you need but to want more than you need. Capitalism is safe. Let the checks be sent out.

Send the money out. Fuck it. Just send them money. It's all these goddamned sticky fingers in between that are getting their hands on the money. Not your goddamned poor people. They aren't getting a fucking goddamned red cent. Mainly what the government supports is the government. I say fuck 'em. Let the fucking government go to hell. Look, if you can't absolutely eliminate governments, certainly the one thing you absolutely ought to do is viciously enfeeble them. Now that's a political principle. I call for the vicious enfeeblement of government.

MEE: Well, this is an argument . . .

MUFFIN MAN: Look, I don't care what kind of a goddamned argument it is. I don't care if it's not the goddamned conventional wisdom. So-the-hell what? I've dealt in conventional wisdom for years. Look, I've had jobs, I've met payrolls, I've dealt in the conventional wisdom. I've read the newspapers. I know what their conventional wisdom is. I can spout the conventional wisdom from here until doomsday. What the fuck good does it do? Look, finally, after all is said and done, what the hell good has the conventional wisdom done? To hell with the conventional wisdom. Get away from it. Strike out from it. Go beyond it. So what the hell do you know? All the—what the hell do you know—familiar guideposts go. What are you, afraid you're crazy? Afraid that—I mean all the reference points are gonna disappear, that all of these checkpoints that reassure you that you're sane. But who the hell knows if you're still sane. You may be wrong. Or worse, you may be absolutely completely insane. What the hell. I'd rather be wrong and have tried than be wrong and never have tried at all. What the hell kind of thing are you trying to tell me about? What kind of argument is this? Look, the best hope we've got is if people will simply stop supporting this government. We don't need revolution. Never mind revolution. Never mind rising up in arms. Never mind all that bullshit out of the 1960s. Just kill it.

Just withdraw. Just leave it alone. Just go away. Forget it. Let it die.

MEE: Well, I suppose if you let it die, then there is some possibility of a new life, and bit by bit, as sanity is restored to the government, I suppose people could restore their support for the government and come back into some sort of political community. Maybe that's the way to bring about the renaissance.

MUFFIN MAN: The what?

MEE: The renaissance.

MUFFIN MAN: A renaissance?

MEE: Right.

MUFFIN MAN: You're really fucking crazy.

Four

I N the summer of 1953, on a July Saturday morning, I was a young golden boy, football-basketball-baseball playing, high-hurdle-jump-ing swimmer standing at the end of a high dive where I hesitated a moment, reaching around to massage the small of my back, feeling a slight ache, a stiffness, the residue, I thought fleetingly, of the bad wrench I had given my back in a football game long ago the previous autumn, twisting for an extra inch or two after I had been tackled and then being twisted at

the bottom of a pileup. I dived from the high board,
a one-and-a-half forward flip. I was too slow, too stiff,
and, when I hit the water, badly, I wrenched my back.
I got out of the water, finding it hard to stand straight.
My legs seemed a bit tired too, I noticed, and now—
the result, no doubt, of too much sun, too much water,
and my back strain—I had a headache. I lay down. I
did not feel well. My stomach, too, for some reason, did
not feel well. It did not feel exactly upset; it just
did not feel well. And I was tired.

I went home, feeling my eyes had been too much
in the sun, sensing that everything seemed slightly
bleached, and I lay down for a few hours to rest. I had
to rest. And to feel well that evening, for that evening
I had a date with a girl whom I had loved and longed
for and thought beautiful for a very long time. Her
name was Stephanie; she was called Stevie; and she
had finally come around to take a small interest in
me. We were to go to a dance at the country club
that evening, a formal dance with dinner and with
some swimming in the evening, with candlelit tables
around the swimming pool Afterward, I had finally
decided, I would hold Stevie and kiss her and perhaps, I
thought weakly, put my hand on her breast. I had not
ever put my hand on a girl's breast. This was to be
the night that I lost, as I thought of it, my virginity,
or at least most of it.

In the early evening, I rose slowly from my bed, I
showered slowly, not understanding why I did not feel
refreshed. I dressed lethargically in a white summer

jacket, the then-fashionable plaid bow tie. I felt well-pressed, well-starched, and weak. I would have to coast. I would have to idle. I would have to be cool and drift through the evening, never expending an ounce of strength unnecessarily. When an occasion arose for laughter, I decided, I would have to make do with a well-projected quiet smile. If excitement were called for, I would have to summon up all the sparkle I had and concentrate it in my eyes and try to communicate it that way.

I moved somnambulistically through the evening, eating little, speaking little, swimming not at all, but dancing much, staying on my feet, moving, trying to work the ache out of my legs. I did not believe in giving in to such things as aches. The thing to do with an ache was to lean into it, push it, master it. It may be that by pushing myself I made it worse. After the dance, I took Stevie home. Someone had a car. Someone drove. One or two other couples were with us. We would all go to Stevie's home and there, with records and Cokes, I would kiss Stevie. We got out of the car, and I could not be sure if I was able to focus on the house. I was perspiring; my legs were weak; I was beginning to weave. I got to the door and could go no further. I held on to the door jamb to keep from falling down. Everyone else was already inside. The room began to bleach out into white; I was fainting; and I commenced to mumble something.

They turned to look at me. I hadn't the strength to complete the sentence. I had to save my energy to keep from falling down, but I rallied for a moment. and mumbled again—I don't know what.

I could not make the proper apologies. I was too sick and confused. I turned, seeing, as I turned, Stevie's look of confusion and hurt. She was too hurt even to come to the door, to ask whether I needed help. She stood, stunned, rooted, dismayed. I turned and started to walk out across her lawn. I heard the voices of other boys asking if I were all right, whether I needed a ride, and again I mumbled, again I don't remember quite what it was, but I reassured them that I was fine. Someone offered me a ride in a car, but I said, "No thanks. I just need some fresh air. I'd rather walk."

And so I walked home. It took a while. I felt weak, and I was weaving quite a bit now. I found that if I leaned forward my momentum would carry me and then I had only to throw my feet loosely out ahead for support. I missed a couple of times and fell and knew I must be more careful, for if I fell again, I knew I would not be able to get up.

At home, my parents awoke, or had been still awake, and called out a hello to me. My response must have sounded strange, because they asked if I was all right. I said I was, that I'd had a good time. I tried to be quiet, but an hour or two later I awakened my parents again. I was walking around, trying to walk through the ache and subdue it.

I had begun by now to lose consciousness in any ordinary sense. The slight fever just beginning to rise along with the ache, the nausea, the preoccupation with the way I had hurt Stevie's feelings, had failed to kiss her, had not been a good social creature, all combined to screen off my parents' call to the doctor, the trip in the car (I was now lying across the back seat) to the hospital, being wheeled down the tiled corridors, lifted onto a bed somewhere, nurses and orderlies poking and worrying and fussing, all uncertain and inefficient, and then, suddenly, the apparition of the red-headed nurse, Mrs. Fuller, mother of two professional football players, big, tough, gentle, no bullshit woman, the head nurse. She appeared, and the nurses, orderlies, and residents parted. She walked up to the side of my bed, looked directly into my eyes, and said, "This boy has polio."

She reached down and scooped me up, this fourteen-year-old 160-pound boy, picked me up in her arms, hugging me and holding me, and carried me back down a long, long corridor all by herself, into a corridor less brightly lit, a corridor that seemed cool and quiet, into the isolation ward, into a single room there, and placed me in the bed.

It is difficult to write about these events now without romanticizing and without self-pity and without, no doubt, a number of other peculiar emotions that the reader will recognize before I do, because, to me, these events were all crucially important; they changed my life, and, speaking coolly, it does seem a pity to cut down a strong and healthy boy at the age of puberty. Is the suggestion of rage apparent? I shall not, as Dylan Thomas advised, go gently into that good night. When I am not too angry, I try to recall a passage from that great indiscriminate seeker of experiences, Henry Miller. I try to accept this passage of Miller's with equanimity: "We have all met the soldier who has been overseas. And we all know that each one has a different story to relate. We are all like returned soldiers. We have all been somewhere, spiritually speaking, and we have either benefited by the experience or been worsted by it. One man says: 'Never again!' Another says: 'Let it come! I'm ready for anything!' Only the fool hopes to repeat an experience; the wise man knows that *every* experience is to be viewed as a blessing. Whatever we try to deny or reject is precisely what we have need of; it is our very need which often paralyzes us, prevents us from welcoming a (good or bad) experience."

I lay on my back for weeks, dying, in delirium from the fever, my nerves expiring bundle by bundle, screeching out of existence as though they were being ripped out of my body, one by one and all at once. My muscles contracted more and more tightly until they were all as rigid as the grain in a piece of mahogany. I was not simply dying; I was being tortured to death. In a very few days, in perhaps no more than forty-eight hours, I think I learned everything there is to know about controlling and enduring pain, by relaxing into it.

I imagined myself a captive of diabolical enemy

soldiers who were torturing me, trying to get me to give up—what?—to give up living, trying to get me to die voluntarily. I relaxed. I would outwait them. Then, when they let down their guard, I would come back fighting. But first I just learned to relax; I could outwait anyone, anything. At first I could not feel or move my feet or my legs, then the pain blotted out my torso, my back, my chest, my arms, and I felt it working up to blot out my face—and then I knew I would be dead. I needed to do only one thing: keep my nose out where it could get air, keep breathing regularly and calmly.

After this, yoga would have nothing to teach me about the conscious control of my body or about the way in which one can quiet the mind so that it barely ripples along the levels of consciousness. I drew down into myself, very deeply, where I found a very hard, mean, determined will, and there I stayed, counting on it. With the fever, with the heat of summer, I perspired. (Horses sweat, Nan told me, people perspire.) I lost a third of my weight—dropping from 160 to 100 pounds in a week. My body evaporated, dematerialized, and I lay perspiring and delirious and listened to the shrieks of the man down the hall. This man, I learned, had been burned when a furnace blew up in his face. He was so burned that his flesh came off in charred chunks. He could do nothing but beg for shots of heroin. His very existence hurt him; just lying on the sheets was so painful that he evidently thought someone was torturing him, and he moaned and wailed and cried out through the day and night, "Oh, no, please. No. Don't. Oh, no, please. Please don't."

Meanwhile, no one was helping me. No one seemed to know quite what to do. Yet it was clear to everyone that I was dying. I was also, whether or not the doctors and nurses knew it, hallucinating. When, years later, a younger generation would discover the wonders of hallucination, I would be noncommittally self-satisfied, having been there before and very deeply, with visions of heaven and hell, with visions of dying nerves the size of galaxies, visions of fighting off car- toon images left over from World War II, of Japanese soldiers, who savaged me with bayonets and fires and molten iron, visions of beautiful Stephanie, horrified by the ravaged, bleeding, splayed, crippled unmanned young man she might have loved.

It was then that I tried to masturbate, and failed. And perhaps this is the event my neurons recalled to me when I imagined being held powerless in San Clemente by Nixon. It would be weeks before there was any sensation again in my groin, and there is no question that that lack of sensation terrified me; but, I should not exaggerate that fear, since what I was most terrified of, at that moment, was not the loss of my promising manhood, but the loss of life altogether. Later, much later, I would return to these moments and hours and days and wonder at leisure about the timing of this disease, cutting my legs out from under me just as I was entering manhood, and leading me to wonder often whether the disease was not psychosomatic.

Then, happily, a daydream, light, and airy and sweet: Some of my friends came by to see me and to suggest that we all go out for a chocolate malted milk. Bill Dow was there. I was pleased that Bill Dow seemed to be offering his friendship; we had been football players together; we had liked one another well enough but had never been close friends; now Bill seemed quite cordial and friendly; he had suggested the idea that everyone go out for malts. Would I like to go out? Sure. Why not? It was my last carefree act. I swung myself out of bed, somehow, and collapsed to the floor, face down and, now, no longer able to raise my head.

My left arm had been the culprit. My left arm was not yet, at the time of this dream, completely deadened. I had had enough strength apparently to throw myself out of bed with just this one arm. I was evidently eager to get out of that hospital, eager to get back to my old life, my normal life of friends and chocolate malts and ease of getting out and going.

Now, lying face down on the floor, I felt nauseated. Something was clearly very wrong. I lay on dozens and dozens of brightly colored spinning disks; I had to keep them all in balance, all in precise whirling, spinning orbit. By shifting my weight ever so slightly this way or that, if I relaxed for a moment, if I allowed the disks to get even a millimeter out of synchronization, the whole universe would spin off into chaos and I, with the scattered, skittering disks, would be thrown off into the void. I called out for help, but I knew that my voice made no sound. I worked, I perspired. I worked, and shifted my weight, moving myself around as best I could with my one weakening arm, and I perspired. I wished I could cry, but I knew I could not allow myself that luxury. I needed to stay alert, and fighting. In a while, a nurse came into the room—and screamed, and turned around and ran out again. She had thought I was dead.

At last the orderlies came and, finding that I was still alive, put me back in my bed, and put bars around my bed so that I could not get out again. By then, however, the bars were not necessary. By then my left arm was dead. I could move nothing but a few fingers on my left hand. There I lay, thinking.

When a boy or man is at his nadir, on the edge of death, with nothing to hang on to, what does his parish priest do? His parish priest comes by and nudges that man or boy toward death. So it seemed, in any event, to me. There I lay, my body vanishing in fever and delirium, with a man down the hall wailing, "Please don't, oh please stop," when who should appear in my room but the Reverend Alexander N. Thane, wondering whether I would like to make a last confession before I received Extreme Unction. A last confession! The bastards!

My self-pity turned to rage, and I wished to tear apart the hospital and murder the priest and curse God and destroy the world. But, fuck it, I could not afford to waste the smallest part of my strength. I wished Father Thane would just go away and not tempt me to spend my last strength in anger and so die. I found within myself a kind of self-control that I imagined was more powerful than any millions of adults ever dreamed of having. I replied very quietly and calmly to the priest, "No, thank you, Father."

And so, the Reverend Thane gave me Extreme Unction anyway.

From the Reverend Thane's point of view, this was a good thing to do. My soul was prepared for death, for heaven, prepared to meet God. From my point of view, this was a bad thing: To me, it was immediately clear that the Church was finished with me. All they cared was to see to the performance of the prescribed ritual; they did not care, in fact, whether I lived or died. Very well, let me be dead as far as the Church is concerned. And let the Church be dead as far as I was concerned. Fair enough. It was a deal. I was content. I was finished with the Church. Done, and done. Fuck it. Amen.

Such bitter rage was tolerable against the Church, but who had called the priest? My father had called the priest. Thus, I reasoned, my father, a good man, was trying to do everything he thought best for his son, and this calling of the priest must be a good thing, since my father had called the priest. And yet, given the choice between staking absolutely everything on the life of his son, calling in every specialist as far away as China, leaving no stone unturned to ensure his son's life, given that choice, the father hedged his bets and called in the priest. Why did my father not tear down the walls of the hospital, scream at all the priests to stay away, shout to the world that his son would live, damn it, or he would curse God and all creation forever? Why had he not staked everything on life for his son, gambled all for that life? Why not? Here is the origin of a special rage against my father that I did not allow myself to recognize for many years and so gave myself and my father a good bit of needless anguish. In time, I came, I think, to understand my father. My father had indeed and of course called for specialists all around, had wept and raged —out of my presence, so as not to alarm me. But I did not come to understand my father before I had lodged some bits and pieces of vengeance against him for this presumed betrayal of me, not until I had inflicted wounds upon my father, not understanding why I was doing so, feeling guilty for doing so, and wishing to hurt my father even more.

Father Thane was not alone in his wishing a good death on me. My father had brought in platoons of private nurses to watch over me around the clock, and one of these nurses was a devout Catholic woman, who always entered my room choking back tears. This woman—no doubt a fine and generous woman, for all nurses who worked with polio victims risked contracting polio themselves—brought in holy medals and scapular medals, and other religious whatnots each time she appeared on duty. It soon became evident that a race was on between her supply of holy medals and my date of death. She would bring them into the room and place them on my bed, all around the edges at first, and then closer and closer to me, touching my hands and my fingers, until I looked like the garishly decorated corpse of a saint along the wall of an Italian church. I would ask her to take them away, but she would not. She would put them next to my hands, as though I were holding them, as though I wanted to hold them, and, when she was out of the room, I would strain until tears came to my eyes, trying to move my hand away from these holy medals, and unable to move my hand even a thousandth of an inch.

I bore up under this treatment for days, because I knew this woman was only doing what she thought best, and because I knew she had a generous heart, and I could not be such a rotten, angry ingrate as to object to her form of loving generosity. But at last I could bear it no longer, and one day, after my father, wearing a white gown, white cap, white mask, and standing off at a distance from the bed, asked me whether there was anything he could do for me, I said yes. Yes, he could please take away those holy medals.

Now, the remarkable thing about death is that it is really a wonderful thing, provided that there is an afterlife. There is no question that I had died. I had been given the sacrament of Extreme Unction, which proved it. And it is, for a boy, interesting to die. While on the one hand I may have salted away a few debts of revenge, on the other hand, when I woke up to discover that there was another life waiting for me, it turned out that I was much freer and more fearless in some ways than other people. Now, if I meet agents of SMERSH and they threaten to kill me, I can always say, "Go ahead. I'm already dead anyway." The recipient of Extreme Unction may dread pain, but at least in theory, he need have no fear of death, since he has already died and been given passage to heaven.

Moreover, a boy who has died has a chance to be reborn. The experience of being born again is appallingly common these days; and, although I wince when I hear others speak of the event, I suppose it is no less singular an experience for being a universal one. With a boy's rebirth, he can take more risks, since this second life of his is all free—and all his own. This second life is one that he has earned himself. The Church had given up on him (or so, at least, he imagined); and he, in hard, teeth-gritting, concentrated, ruthlessly selfish rage and self-pity, had alone willed himself back to life.

He came back damaged; he came back wounded, muscles wasted, legs immobile; but he came back, able ultimately to walk with the help of a crutch and a cane. Having been written off, having been murdered in some sense, he came back able in some sense to kill. He came back dangerous. And even though he was lying flat on his back, able to move nothing but the fingers of his left hand and his facial muscles, he knew that he must learn to control himself before he got all his strength back, or else he would spring out of bed and murder everyone.

I have slipped into speaking of myself automatically in the third person, because in most respects, this fourteen-year-old boy of whom I speak seems to be less myself as I know myself to be today and more simply a young boy I once knew, whose experiences I have felt intensely, and who remains someone for whom I have a great deal of affection, but who is a boy who is not me. But, of course, I do speak of myself. I remember that as a fifteen-year-old boy, I was complimented by everyone for my good cheer. And I was indeed cheerful, but not too cheerful. I was careful not to fall into the trap of overcompensating. I cried a few times, but only a few times. I would not fall into the trap of self-pity either. I attended very carefully to my emotions, in fact, maintaining myself with great attentiveness as a well-balanced, emotionally stable all-American boy. Everyone marveled at me. I did it by sheer will.

By sheer will, too, I developed an appearance of ease, confidence, a sense of being relaxed, an impression of being in command—and thus, I always felt myself, after having had polio, to be essentially phony. I had begun, without quite knowing it, a truly massive denial of my real feelings, and so while I thought that I had been reborn to a new life, I would, in fact, have to be reborn yet again, later on, into an awareness and acceptance of those feelings. As a matter of fact, rebirth has got to be a habit, and while I recognize several large and traumatic rebirths in my life, the truth is that I seem to be reborn again and again, and I am finally getting to enjoy it and welcome it.

Nonetheless, however self-congratulatory I may become about my talent for birth and rebirth and renewal, the fact of the matter is that polio did either create or intensify a severe fissure in my psyche that, despite innumerable jolly rebirths, persists today. When I was first stricken with polio, and lying on my back in the hospital, it occurred to me that in order to save my life, I needed to exercise that old mind-over-matter trick. However, in thinking that I saved myself by sheer will, I managed to drive a wedge between the physical and the mental world, which is, perhaps, not a very healthy thing for an individual to do.

One begins first by denying the primacy of the physical world, then goes on to deny the force of material reality, and finally moves to the logical conclusion that there is no such thing as material reality, that truth lies not in the material world, but somewhere else. Those who are still blessed with the ability to believe in God believe that truth lies in the spiritual world. Others of us resort to a belief that reality lies in an intellectual world. This is not a bad idea, taken in small doses. But it is a kind of craziness if it becomes monomaniacal and if one begins to insist that this single vision of the world encompasses all reality.

"In the schizoid condition," R. D. Laing has written in *The Divided Self*, ". . . there is a persistent scission between the self and the body. What the individual regards as his true self is experienced as more or less disembodied, and bodily experience and actions are in turn felt to be part of the false-self system. . . . In general, one can say that it is a response that appears to be available to most people who find themselves enclosed within a threatening experience from which there is no physical escape. Prisoners in concentration camps *tried* to feel that way, but the camp offered no possible way out, either spatially or at the end of a period of time. The only way out was by a cyclical withdrawal 'into' oneself and 'out of' the body." The inner self and the outer self that Laing describes, the intellectual, emotional, and physical worlds that have been sundered can be reunited, as the romantics have known all along, and as psychology has confirmed, by love.

Because of the way that the nerves die and the way that the muscles contract from polio, the disease tends to leave its victim as stiff as stiffs at first. Each muscle has to be stretched out again. First the patient is placed in a warm whirlpool bath to be relaxed. Then he's brought out, placed on the table, his legs and arms and torso are pulled and bent and stretched by a therapist. The foot is raised half an inch off the exercise table; the patient grimaces. The other foot is raised half an inch off the exercise table; the patient grimaces. Twice a day, day after day, this goes on—the baths, the stretching, the foot comes up an inch, two inches; the knee is bent, ever so slightly.

With great effort, the patient raises his left hand off the table all by himself and holds it off the table for a few seconds before it drops back of its own weight. He still cannot lift his right hand off the table.

I came to love my therapists. The blonde, middle-aged physically ugly old maid whose mouth slanted strangely to one side (from a stroke? a birth defect?) was firm and demanding and gentle. The older woman with gray streaks in her black hair, diminutive, with a wiry little body, Miss Jones, Jonesie, was more sympathetic, but only a shade more sympathetic. Self-pity was not encouraged in this physical therapy shop. Examples of those who were worse off were daily pointed out. To those who had merely lost the use of an arm, someone flat out was made an example. Those who were flat on their backs were referred to someone in an iron lung. The relatives of someone in an iron lung were told, "It could have been worse. At least he is alive." And the relatives of someone who had died were told, "It could have been worse. He could have survived and spent the rest of his life in an iron lung."

Relativism, it began to occur to me at the age of fourteen, in the grading of physical condition, in the gauging of pain, in the assessment of worth, goodness, happiness, or other life situations, in the evaluation of ethical positions, is bullshit. Life has within it a number of absolute intractable nonrelative facts that cannot be taken back, apologized for, or changed, but that must be dealt with. While I discovered that

I had a remarkable talent for denying emotional reali-
ties that were too monstrously difficult for me to deal
with, I discovered too that I had a certain brutal
courage in addressing myself to facts that others
wished to deny or have me deny. I'm glad that I was
blessed with this ability. It saved me a great deal of
time, and it made life intensely interesting to me. I
discovered that I had a great curiosity and pleasure
in and taste for phenomena. It had dawned on me
that one of the facts of my life was the inability to
walk, run, jump, skip, or play football. I could not
be a professional baseball player. I could not be a
fireman or a policeman or a soldier or a pilot. I could
not stand at a machine to earn my living. I could not
lift heavy things. By a process of elementary elimina-
tion, I was left with only my head to work with. And,
it then occurred to me that my head was empty, or, to
be charitable, very sparsely furnished.

This same thought had apparently occurred to
Miss Maude Strauss, my high school English teacher.
Miss Strauss and I loved each other, although, of
course, neither of us had admitted it to the other. She
appeared one day, standing in the door of my room
at Sherman Hospital. She wore the same old print
dress she always wore. She was built squarely like a
Mack truck, solid. Her hair was black, dyed black,
dyed so many times that it had been turned into
tough little wires that stuck out from her head like
a proto-Afro. She looked like Medusa. She was shy.

She came bearing a book, her very own personal

copy of a book, which had occasional notes and under-linings in her hand, a plain gray paper-cover book, perhaps more of a pamphlet than a book. It was Plato's *Symposium*. I didn't know it at the time, but Maude Strauss was saying that she loved me by giving me this conversation about love.

So many women in my adolescent life were single women—so many teachers, so many nurses, my physical therapist. They were, most of them, old maids, not widows; and it was whispered of some of them that somewhere in the distant past was a lover or a husband, some passionate and tragic affair or marriage. Some of these women surely must have been lesbians; some of them must at least have had difficult psycho-sexual feelings about mature men. They lavished their love, whatever motivated it, whatever diverted it, whatever bent it from its presumably natural course, upon adolescent boys and upon me. And that seemed at the time, and seems in retrospect, a wonderful thing.

Plato's *Symposium* was read and reread and re-read. I did not understand it. I had not yet had time to understand heterosexual love. I did not know that homosexual love existed, except vaguely somewhere in New York. I enjoyed the talk, the logic, the give-and-take, the dialogue, the drama, the tension. In Plato, unlike in the teachings of the Roman Catholic Church, the very style of presentation, the very form of the dialogue conveys an understanding that life is full of, on the one hand, this, and, on the other hand, that, of painful contradiction, of uncertainty, of opposing views and arguments of the very tug and pull of life itself, of the very tug and pull, especially, of life for a fourteen-year-old boy whose feelings about himself and his life were in painful turmoil. Plato spoke to me with a directness, a keenness, an immediacy that no other book had ever done. Before I read Plato, I had read nothing but assigned school texts, and those very inattentively. And comic books. That was all. Now, I devoured Plato.

Soon Miss Strauss returned for another visit. We both understood a little better now that we loved each other. In reading the *Symposium* I had become increasingly sensitive to the underlinings in Miss Strauss's hand. I wondered whether they dated back to old school days or whether she had done this underlining especially for me to convey a message to me about her love for me? I did not dare to ask her, but I told her that I loved the book and that I found in it many of my own feelings. She was flustered. How difficult, and how bizarre, was this tense, unadmitted love affair between the bedridden boy and his aging mistress. She gave me two more books: one that contained Plato's full account of the trial and death of Socrates, the *Apology, Crito, Euthyphro,* and *Phaedo,* as well as *The Republic,* and another that contained Aristotle's brief essay "On Interpretation" and his "Politics."

"Youth," Erik Erikson wrote in *Young Man Luther,* "can be the most exuberant, the most care-

159

less, the most self-sure, and the most unself-consciously productive stage of life, or so it seems if we look primarily at the 'once-born.' This is a term which William James adopted from Cardinal Newman; he uses it to describe all those who rather painlessly fit themselves and are fitted into the ideology of their age, finding no discrepancy between its formulation of past and future than the daily tasks set by the dominant technology.

"James differentiates the once-born from those 'sick souls' and 'divided selves' who search for a second birth, a 'growth crisis' that will 'convert' them in their 'habitual center of . . . personal energy.' He approvingly quotes Edwin D. Starbuck to the effect that 'conversion is in its essence a normal adolescent phenomenon.' . . . What is to be relinquished as 'old' may be the individual's previous life; this usually means the perspectives intrinsic to the lifestyle of the parents, who are thus discarded, contrary to all traditional safeguards of filial devotion. The 'old' may be part of himself . . ."

Those whose first births are not successful, Erikson would say, must be born again. In my own case, this need coincided with reports of my death, which, as it turned out, were not exaggerated. I had especially great need of rebirth. I was forced to it.

I was reborn in books. I was reborn first in philosophy; and I read it all. Within two years, I had sampled every philosopher from Plato to Sartre and I had read almost all of Plato, most of Descartes, much

Hegel and Kierkegaard and James and Santayana and Wittgenstein and Carnap. I had devoured these men; I had sucked them in and absorbed them; and I had debated with them, with that wonderful know-it-all arrogance of youth, on equal terms.

I read for many reasons: First of all, perhaps, because nature abhors a vacuum and my head was a vacuum. Second, I read because I had great need to understand why it was that I had got polio. Third, since God had become intimately mixed up in my daily life, in questions of fairness and life and death, I needed to find out about God. And I moved through the Fathers of the Church with some considerable care and thoroughness. I read them all. I read Aquinas more than a few times, until I had memorized all of his proofs for the existence of God—and disproved them all to my satisfaction. I was no longer objective on the God-question, it is true, but I did try to give God every benefit of the doubt (remarkably generous of me, that) . But, by now, there were too many doubts.

The tortured nature of my theological speculations, mixed up as they were with personal chagrin, disappointment, wrath, psychological turmoil of all sorts, took me, the self-made adventurer, scholar, naturally, into St. Augustine. There, too, I dwelt for a long time reading and rereading the *Confessions,* until I moved gradually out of the confines of the Church into other confessions, autobiographies, biographies, and into histories—the progress begins now to take on the aspects of inevitability—of the Italian

Renaissance. I read of the humanists, of those who left the Church more or less to embrace liberalism, individualism, the pleasures and exhilarations of the world, of the pleasures of art, music, and fine clothes and money and politics, and the cut and thrust and sexy life-enhancing turmoil of daily life. I was reborn into the world, and, in brief, I liked it. Later on, as a grown-up writer and editor, I would write books about Lorenzo di Medici, Erasmus, Pope Leo X and Luther, and about daily life in the Renaissance, and people would wonder at my apparently cool, objective, amateur scholar's interest in this remote historical epoch. Little did they know that these books were all autobiographical, and that to me the Renaissance was nothing but the immediate palpable story of my own life, of my own rebirth, of my own awakening to the richness of life, and that I liked nothing better than to recall it, to touch it again and again, to live through it repeatedly, as misers love to wallow in their gold.

A boy stricken with polio thinks a great deal about power and impotence, strength and weakness, justice and injustice. He wonders in what way all men are created equal, in what their equality resides, and whether or not this equality can be lost, whether some can become, as Orwell's *Animal Farm* would have it, "less equal than others." Now it is obvious, first of all, that this fourteen-year-old boy who came down with polio in 1953 was not equal to other fourteen-year-old boys physically. In the past, when he was thirteen, one might have said he was more or less equal, that differences in physical strength were so minor as to be trivial, but that was no longer the case after 1953. It occurred to the boy that there could be no question either of intellectual equality with others, or of equality of background, wealth, or even, certainly not now, of opportunity.

This, I think, is roughly the process of thought that I went through as a fourteen-year-old boy, as I lay on my back in bed. I wondered: If all people are created equal, in what sense are they created equal? God did not create them equal, for people are not equally endowed at birth. Their parents did not create them equal, for the backgrounds and economic and social lives of parents, the homes in which they raised their children, the expectations they give to their children, the psychological and emotional and intellectual preparation they give their children, are not at all equal. Nor are all people created equal by the world into which they have been born; in fact, the longer they dwell in the world, the more the world or fate or destiny or chance or the designs of others imposes inequalities upon people. Who, or what, creates people equal, then?

Only one thing, I concluded, creates people equal: Only democratic politics creates people equal. And it does create; politics does not recognize an innate or earned equality; politics creates equality, equality before the law. In democratic politics, and in no other politics, people come together and declare themselves and one another to be equal. Henceforth, these people are, politically, equal. They have declared and created themselves equal. By that declaration, and only by that declaration, and only politically, they are equal. By *fiat*. And the *fiat* makes it so.

Who, then, has created people equal? They themselves have done so. And thus we have a definition of politics: Politics is the act of self-creation.

There is no higher act than that of self-creation. It is, of course, God-like, and it gives each person the opportunity to make his own destiny. People can create themselves equal or unequal, noble or ignoble, virtuous or evil, generous or mean-spirited. People make their own politics and live their own politics, whatever political system in which they may find themselves at the moment, however they may choose to accommodate themselves to it, or abandon it. And in making their politics they create themselves, for better or worse.

Two apparently contradictory strains run through politics, it seems to me, as they commenced to run through my own life in the summer of 1953. Those two urges can be reduced to very simple demands that we all make of the world. The first demand that we make is: "Let me be." And the second demand is: "Give me a hand." I certainly made that second demand because, whatever one might say about my emotional, psychological, or philosophical adventures, the fact was that I was once a child who could not help himself and would not have survived without an extraordinary vast welfare state composed of doctors and nurses and hospitals and therapists and dozens of other people and systems and institutions—and parents.

I leave aside those other human urges: the urge to take, to eat, to grab, to kill, to own, to dominate all. All political systems, to be regarded as such in any way, curb those appetites. We esteem democracy because it aspires to curb, and to channel into socially useful directions, the urges of everyone, whereas monarchies or tyrannies or oligarchies aspire to curb the urges of everyone except the monarch or the tyrant or the oligarchs. The point is self-evident, and politics only becomes intellectually interesting when it attempts to deal with our more complex urges.

My urge to be treated as someone free and equal to others, an urge that was perhaps made even more passionate after I was stricken with polio, is the sort of urge that one ordinarily expects to find embraced by those defenders of individualism and liberty, the old Republican party, and such writers as Robert Nisbet and Hannah Arendt. And that other need, for help, is a need that has generally been answered by the old Democratic party, by those writers who address themselves to issues of social justice, the problems of poverty.

These two urges, for liberty and for social justice, appear to many who think about politics, to be naturally antagonistic concerns, possibly even mutually exclusive ones. Hannah Arendt, for example, wrote that any politics addressed to the material needs of the people, to filling bellies, is inherently foredoomed to undermine liberty, because, she believed, any politics that is responsive to necessity will always have need, never liberty, at its core. Arendt was not happy about poverty, or indifferent to the toll poverty takes. On the contrary, "poverty is more than deprivation," she wrote, "it is a state of constant want and acute misery whose ignominy consists in its dehumanizing force; poverty is abject because it puts men under the absolute dictate of their bodies, that is, under the absolute dictate of necessity as all men know it from their most intimate experience and outside all speculations. It was under the rule of this necessity that the multitude rushed to the assistance of the French Revolution, inspired it, drove it onward, and eventually sent it to its doom, for this was the multitude of the poor. When they appeared on the scene of politics, necessity appeared with them, and the result was that the power of the old regime became impotent and the new republic was stillborn; freedom had to be surrendered to necessity, to the urgency of the life process itself."

The problem of poverty, Arendt insisted, is a problem that must be solved by technology, not by politics. Arendt believed that the unique good luck of the United States when it was founded was that it was an abundant country and that therefore our Founding Fathers could, for the most part, neglect those issues of social justice and devote themselves to questions of political liberty. Arendt believed this was not only a blessing for the United States, but also an

absolute precondition for the securing of political
liberty. "Nothing, we might say today, could be more
obsolete than to attempt to liberate mankind from
poverty by political means; nothing could be more
futile and more dangerous." For, Arendt believed:
"The whole record of past revolutions demonstrates
beyond doubt that every attempt to solve the social
question with political means leads into terror, and
that it is terror which sends revolutions to their doom
. . . what has always made it so terribly tempting to
follow the French Revolution on its foredoomed path
is not only the fact that liberation from necessity,
because of its urgency, will always take precedence
over the building of freedom, but the even more important and more dangerous fact that the uprising of
the poor against the rich carries with it an altogether
different and much greater momentum of force than
the rebellion of the oppressed against their oppressors.
This raging force may well nigh appear irresistible
because it lives from and is nourished by the necessity of biological life itself ('the rebellions of the belly
are the worst,' as Francis Bacon put it). . . ."

Other political philosophers, of course, write of
the need to dedicate politics to the aim of establishing
and ensuring social justice: To ignore the ravages of
poverty is to ignore the most obviously pressing human
need, to which all efforts should be bent to answer.
What other earthly goal is worth pursuing?

I could not get over the simpleminded feeling, as
I lay in bed thinking of Plato and Aristotle and my

own needs, that somehow a massive false argument had got started, that we had all been distracted for the past decades by a phony issue, and the Founding Fathers had been straightforwardly and simply correct in dedicating their country to both liberty and justice for all.

If democracy can only work with citizens who have full bellies, then bellies must be filled so that all citizens may act freely; then, and only then, may democracy begin to work. Full bellies are a precondition of liberty, not an alternative goal. If all citizens do not have full bellies, democracy does not and cannot exist, and thus none of us can be free. Equality is a precondition for liberty—and that is why we create ourselves equal, so that we may be free.

We ought to stop trying to manipulate poverty and the poor, stop trying to "improve" poor people with welfare payments, stop trying to oversee what they do with their money, stop using poverty as an excuse to build a massive federal bureaucracy, and just hand out money to all the poor as quickly and efficiently as possible—with one large computer that writes its own checks—not because the poor deserve it, but because democracy, our own liberty, requires it.

I got out of the hospital in the autumn of 1953. I was, by that time, able to walk with crutches and a leg brace—but only on very smooth surfaces. It would take me half an hour to walk just a short distance down a hospital corridor, my feet sliding on the highly polished floor. I could not manage getting up and down steps, and the thought of having to navigate a concrete sidewalk, with its rough texture, was bleakly defeating. But my sister Elizabeth had read a lot of Janet Lambert books, and she knew just how to treat me. She treated me like a returning war hero. It had exactly the right mix of everything, this style of treatment. It made me feel special. It made me feel as though I had been through a great searing experience. It made me feel heroic. It forced me to deny any feelings of self-pity I might have. And it forced me, too, to think of my returning home as the beginning of a new life. I had seen war movies, and I knew what happened next. Next, the war hero worked himself back into the ordinary conduct of life and, if he remained cheerful and was not bitter, he lived happily ever after. My sister managed also to interpose herself between myself and my parents.

My parents, as one might have expected, wished to take care of me and pamper me and coddle me—and they did, and I loved it. But my sister made sure that this sort of thing did not go on endlessly, to my great relief, and possibly even to the great relief of my parents. My childhood friends came by to visit. Stephanie came by for a visit. She was wonderful and sweet and friendly and wanted to have nothing to do with me anymore. I might be a war hero, but she wanted that season's left halfback. Jim Condill, my old basketball-playing buddy, came by often. And we, who had been friends for life, remained friends for life. We who had run and jumped and played ball together and gone on double dates together, bicycled together, remained inseparable pals. Jim made my re-entry into that day-to-day life—I cannot say easier—I must say possible. He took a great interest in my newfound intellectual endeavors; and I took a great interest in his continuing athletic prowess. He was a terrific basketball player, and I became, I think, one of his greatest fans. We were a good complementary pair for one another. I was the introvert, he the extrovert. I, the bookish man. He, the man of the world. As we grew up, these character traits manifested themselves in our adult lives. I grew up to be an editor, leaning over a desk, pushing a pencil, fiddling with manuscripts, exhausting my eyes. He grew up to be a salesman, out in the world, meeting people, drinking and dining. We had, as young adolescents, one of those perfect young male adolescent relationships of mutual support and respect and admiration and love. We hardly ever see each other anymore, but when we do, we resume our conversation just where we left off. Jim is involved with a family growing up now. And so he has lost, just as I have, some of the taste for adolescent stupidity that we used to share. But he has aged well, and we have not grown apart. If ever I desperately need help, and all my other friends have abandoned me, I'll phone Jim. If ever I was to go mad and wind up in an asylum, not at all sure what I thought anymore or who I was, in order to find out, I'd call Jim. If ever I needed to check my political beliefs and make sure they were still in touch with reality, I'd call Jim. If ever I was to run for political office, the first person I'd call would be Jim. And, when I end up a man in his eighties, looking for agreeable companionship, and most of the people I've known in my life have died, I'll call Jim.

After polio came the cover-up. I could not face the pain I felt at being—a word I could not even speak for twenty years—crippled; I could not face being, as I imagined I was, something less than a whole man; I could not console myself that others had had to learn to live without an arm or a leg or sight or hearing or speech. I raged against my fate, raged in a horrendous bellowing screaming silence—all the while I smiled and was relaxed and at ease.

I covered up, too, the cover-up, covered up the rage, covered up my homicidal urges, my wish to kill my doctors, my nurses, that priest who gave me Extreme Unction, my father, and Thomas Aquinas. I admitted to no feelings of pettiness, nastiness, meanness, self-pity, wishes to get even, to get revenge, to hurt in small ways, I admitted no disappointment and no loss.

Instead, I screwed myself determinedly into my vision of a normal life and tried to keep my rage transmogrified into a burning ambition. That ambition churned and screeched and boiled and threatened to go zapwinging off into fierce directions, and I had to watch it, hold it back, battle it, restrain it, make sure the driving force of rage did not break through the social convention of ambition and murder someone.

I read books, and I learned the gift of gab. I discovered that I could so amaze my contemporaries with talk of Goethe or Spinoza that they altogether forgot —or so I imagined—my ever-present crutches. I faced certain problems. For instance: I did not want anyone to perform certain helpful acts for me. If I was helped in certain ways—if a door was opened for me, for example—that meant I was not able to open the door, which meant that I was handicapped, which meant that I was less than a whole young man—an idea unacceptable to me. But everyone was helpful. How to keep people from helping? I could not say, "Here, I'll get that door," for they would quicken their steps (leaving me behind) and say, "No, never mind, I've got it." I could not say, "Get your filthy fucking hand off that door, shithead." That would have seemed impolite. I had to stop them without their knowing. And so I talked. I fascinated my companions. I held my companions spellbound with amusing stories or arcane knowledge until they had quite forgotten the door and then—I got there first! I opened the door!

I covered up these motivations, covered up the wellsprings of my ambitions, and went fiercely onward, wondering why, from time to time, I had an awesome wish to give it all up, forget it all, throw off the burden. I had wanted once to be a lawyer, but now my socially acceptable goals and behavior began to pall on me. I no longer wished to be polite—my depths of rage would out somehow—and I preferred to be roughhewn and rude; I preferred to say fuck and shit as often as I could in conversation. In high school, I stayed just within the bounds of convention—proving to myself and to my father (I always assumed my mother's acceptance and love) that I could do it, I could have a successful, conventional life. My life in athletics was finished, but I careened into the French Club, the Chess Club, the Masque and Wig, the Honor Society, the National Thespian Society, the Natural History Club, the Round Table Discussion Club and Debating Society. For a time, because of my physical clumsiness, I tried to cultivate grace in my arms and hands, my way of standing, my manner of speaking and writing; but none of this came out graceful; it came out, instead, self-conscious and affected.

I was, withal, still, a master politician—vice-president and president of the school student council and of the large district council that embraced northern Illinois—and I ran for president of the Illinois State Student Council Association. I was defeated for that, and I wondered why. In the back rooms of that convention, after the votes were in, the committees were up to other business, and the politicking resumed in anticipation of the next year; I heard someone say why I had lost: The delegates had a sense that I was too "foxy." *Vox populi, vox Dei.*

I kept up appearances in high school. On Sundays

I went to church with my father. But the moment I got away to Harvard, I never went to church again. I dropped out of the conventional life. I was still frightened enough to wish to maintain a good academic standing; I worked hard in fits and starts to make sure I could still get on the Dean's List at will. I could hang in there. They could not kick me out. I let my hair grow long—this was in the fifties—and I took up with the theater crowd. I lost my interests in theology and philosophy and turned instead to literature—and to the theater, that arena of warring passions and voices that seemed to be my natural life. I acted in plays—to hell with it, I played old men—and directed plays, and wrote plays.

No, I did not quite drop out, for still the fear could grip me from time to time. I did not drop out. Rather I flung myself here and there, desperately, trying to satisfy all contradictory demands at once: on the Dean's List, off the Dean's List, good grades, but not too good, but not too bad either, rebellious but not revolutionary, cutting out but hanging in, playing it close, being foxy, and drinking. I carried around a pint bottle, like any resident-in-good-standing of the Bowery, in my tweed jacket pocket, and I drank—. what the hell, why not, who wants to challenge me?

And I married. Fast. My wife had to be beautiful, and she was, Claire Lu, very beautiful, with widely spaced deep brown eyes, high cheekbones, lovely lips, and a lovely willowy body. She always feared that she was too broad in the hips, too heavy in the thighs, but she was not; she merely gave the barest hint of ampleness to soften her slender body. She was beautiful.

By then, the cover-up that had begun to hide just one or two small facts had necessarily spread to hide more and more of my life from me. Any bit of my past, or present, had come to threaten opening up all the rest of my life to me, to opening up the secrets I could not bear to know, and so I closed off more and more of life until, at last, I had become a smiling, knowledgeable, efficient, respectable, and—for some hours of the day at least—sober functionary.

I had succeeded, had I not, in recovering from polio, succeeded to the extent that I now received compliments that turned at once to ashes: "Yeah, it's too bad you got polio, but in a way it was a blessing, wasn't it? I mean, otherwise you wouldn't have read all those books."

I simplify and distort, to be sure. Lives do not grow and change in quite this way. We think that we are living with, or living down, one problem, while all along we have grown into another one—as I had grown, without quite knowing it, into the problems of my first marriage. Some of the bits and pieces of my old life were dropping away; some of the old rages were subsiding; I was coming to understand, here and there, one part or another of my past, while, at the same time, a new present and future were shaping themselves around me, and being shaped by me.

History works in the same way that the changes in our lives occur. History has no moments that can truly be called turning points—or precious few, in any case. Occasionally an earthquake occurs; occasionally we are injured or stricken ill; but, for the most part, what matters is the effect these events have on our lives, and that effect is shaped by what has gone before and what comes after and what we do. No one can quite say just when or how his individual traits of steadfastness or timidity were formed, just when his character sealed his fate. No one can quite say just when Rome began to take on the aspect of a powerful empire or just when it began to decline. The stuff of our lives and of history is constantly dissolving and coalescing, an infinity of shifting variables appearing and disappearing and coming suddenly into surprising combinations, critical masses.

I don't know just when I recovered from my childhood encounter with polio. I recovered some bits of my health and strength even before Mrs. Fuller lay me down in the isolation ward, many more bits from time to time over the years, and some I have not recovered yet. At some times, I felt surges of new strength and life—usually when I felt love for, and love in return from, a woman; and I have been given great measures of new life and confidence from my children, and I have found reserves of strength each time that I have been able to look back, as though back down into a vast, dark chasm, at my past, and hold my gaze there, if only for a moment, from time to time, without blinking

Nations, too, like people, become sick; civilizations

decline; republics die. They die by degrees, usually, unless they are suddenly destroyed by war or catastrophe; and they recover by degrees, too. They recover as people recover, in bits and pieces, here and there, now and then. They commence to reconstitute themselves, to be reborn, even as they are dying, so that the processes of death and rebirth are simultaneous and perpetual.

It is not written in heaven that all nations that have been republics will be reborn as republics. They can revive as tyrannies, as despotisms, for a time if not forever; they can sink into a long dark period before the forces of vitality and beauty come back. The process is not mystical, but it is mysterious and elusive because it depends upon such evanescent phenomena as faith and honesty and patience and the character of the people. The rebirth of the American Republic, which is even now occurring, will come to pass—because no other form of government finally works very well. The Republic will be reborn—because America's democratic tradition is old and deeply ingrained in the people—but it is not possible to say when.

Five

I rented a fine, swift, shiny, red Mustang from the Hertz thieves at the Beverly Wilshire Hotel and drove sleekly away on that balmy Friday evening, to go up into the Beverly Hills hills above Hollywood to see Beatrice. Beatrice is an old friend of mine, a woman I've known for almost twenty years, a wellborn nattily educated lady from the East, but straight, without edge, quick and bright, unflappable and soothing. She had been the good friend of a college friend, and then a sometime acquaintance in the sixties in New York, someone I saw from time to time at cocktail parties and spoke with for long stretches of the evening; she had drifted to Los Angeles, writing poetry and short stories and, now, film scripts, and when I was calling people to join the committee to impeach Nixon, I had been in touch with her. She labored for some other, local impeachment drive, but we had stayed in touch. We had, over the years, grown close to one another, become intimate without ever making love. I daydreamed about it often enough, vaguely, without much sense of intention, faithful to my marriage. Now, driving up into the hills to her house, I wondered about her.

I had not been to California since the late sixties, since I had gone as an inquisitive editor to see the Hippies, and since then, California had meant nothing to me but sex and liberation, dropping out, smoking dope, getting high, letting go, making love. I would have daydreamed idly of making love with Beatrice even if I had been meeting her in Des Moines, but meeting her in California triggered recollections of imagined Haight-Ashbury orgies.

The orgies of Haight-Ashbury, though they are creatures only of my imagination, call up the whole of the sixties for me. The sixties started well, as a time full of hope, good cheer, beaming expectations. Possibility quickened the decade: possibility for fun, for excitement, for beginnings, for money on the stock market, for fast cars and civil rights, hot popular music and a witty young President. The world offered the prospect of wonderful progress in every way. The universe was subject to complex but understandable networks of perceived or man-made laws that were rational, tractable, and predictable, and all predictions were cheerful.

This cheerfulness was the result of reliance on the efficacy of reason, humanism, liberalism and the natural progress that these all made under the proper conditions for capital investment. These were the compensations for the postponement of immediate gratification; these were the rewards for planning ahead, the application of computer programming and technological vigor; in sum, this was what good boys got if they behaved themselves, worked hard, and kept their hair neatly trimmed.

The rewards of self-discipline were manifest: a B.A. degree, a job, the beginning of a good career. (U 2 kn ern mo pay.) So I repressed my urges toward juvenile delinquency; I repressed the wish to shove it. I identified with John Kennedy. I identified with his Catholicism (knowing he must not really believe that stuff any more than I did); I identified with his Irish name; I identified with his years at Harvard; I identified with his injured back; I identified, too, with his taking of speed, for I, too, in those days of moving along, was just beginning to ingest quantities of bennies and dexies and other tabs and capsules and whatnot; I identified with his vitality; I identified with his rumored sexual appetites; and, most of all, I identified with his worldliness, with his assumption that what mattered in life was wheeling and shaking in the public arena. Me and Jack Kennedy, we were world beaters: with our bad backs and Harvard degrees, our quickness to ferret out the political angle, to spot other good political operators, our desire to hoard compensations, our drive, our stamina, our capacity to outlast all others, to overcome by surviving, by hanging on, by having the last play, and our wit, our self-deprecating wit, the sharpness of our sense of humor, and our stylish friends, our gift for the rousing speech, the soaring phrase, the dream to lift the spirits of others and of ourselves, we had that, Kennedy and I.

The road wound up around the hills and houses, bungalows nestled into the hillsides, and, below, now far below, through the evening dusk, the lights of Hollywood effervesced around the searchlights that boomed the opening of yet another movie at the Oriental Theater. I felt, suddenly, as though I, too, might be made of Celluloid, turned into a bit of instant Hollywood make-believe, as though I had been transformed, in my red Mustang, into a snippet of film in an old thirties romance.

I parked the car just off the road, hugging the hillside, and walked down and down several hundred stone steps that meandered down along the hillside through flowers and ground-cover vines and other strange West Coast vegetation to Beatrice's house, snug and airy, hidden and exposed, private and open to the small garden and the evening, the valley and the night sky.

She wore a simple, soft, clinging acrylic dress, with a high neckline and a full, swirling skirt that communicated her quick movements through the living room, and out onto the terrace, showing me the evening, back again through the living room, which was at once ordered and casual, rich in books and drawings and pottery, comfortable chairs, a soft-woven Indian rug, a warm Scotch blanket, magazines, flowers here and there. Our hands and fingers touching lightly, we kissed without thinking and then felt awkward, my fingers brushed back a few strands of her hair, she touched my cheek, and we kissed again, easily, warmly, affectionately, and moved to the kitchen, where the walls were covered in copper-bottomed pots and pans, dried herbs hanging near the stove, a working kitchen that had been well worked, everything designed to be near at hand, and open windows and a door there, too, leading out into the garden at the rear of the house. She made tea, and I got out the big pottery mugs, and we sat in the kitchen at the large, round oak table, and she looked very good.

I heard no children; I sensed no husband in the house; we sat, I knew, in the middle of a somehow splintered household—but, then, that was certainly familiar. We sat amid the fragments of two nuclear families. The thought tumbled about in my mind. We sat amid the shards of Victorian civilization, or (try again), we sat amid the shards of the world our parents, children of the Victorians, had fashioned. We sat at the center of a world of disintegration. We had,

Beatrice and I, both left our disintegrating churches long since, both left our disintegrating jobs in disintegrating businesses in disintegrating urban areas in a disintegrating economy amid the disintegrating institutions of a disintegrating civilization. What I could not figure out, however, was why, after all this, we both felt so good. I looked at Beatrice; she was quite beautiful. We were, both of us, contented; we felt easy and happy and excited. Altogether, life was good.

We were both, in our incipient middle ages, still children of the sixties, direct descendants of the drugs and the fervent politics, the fear and the rage, of fine high times and of hope running amok. The idyl of the sixties did not last long. As it turned out, the decade began in earnest not with any of the good news, not with Kennedy's election, not with my new career as an editor, not with the first production of a play of mine, not even with my marriage or with the birth of my daughter in October of 1963—but, in November of 1963, with the assassination of Kennedy. I was very disappointed when he was shot. I took it personally. It turned out that the sixties was not epitomized by Kennedy and me working our way successfully out into the public arena, identifying ourselves with the great issues of the world, participating in a larger and happy life. No, the sixties really commenced with the assassination of Kennedy, and it became the decade of smash-ups and dashed hopes. The public world, the larger life, the place in which good boys take their appointed stations, was shattered.

I rejected the theories that attempted to explain Kennedy's death as the result of a well-planned conspiracy. Those theories, I thought, were merely trying to console frightened mortals with the thought that the end of a life could be explained in rational ways. But no, I thought no: There is no explanation; the best laid plans can be destroyed by accident, by quirk, by chance, in an instant. Not even his money, not even his political connections, not even his father could save him. I did not realize it, but I had already begun, however young and unpracticed a dramatist I may have been, to make all the world my stage, peopling it with facets of my own character and history, my wishes and dreads. I mourned for both Kennedy and myself, the death of my own hopes, the end of my own career as a touch-football player.

Careers were not what they had been cracked up to be, I found—no, nor marriages either. My efforts to step out into the world were awkward and stumbling in the extreme. Everything was going to be much harder than anyone had mentioned, and I was ill-prepared. I had thought I had paid my dues; I had thought it was time to collect. Instead, entropy had set in. The world was coming apart, and so was I.

I knew something of twentieth-century philosophy, something of science, and accepted the conclusions, or tendencies, of both in a cool, half-attentive sort of way. But the death of Kennedy finally made all these abstractions inescapable for me. His assassination proved to me that life was irretrievably unpredictable, that the world and its inhabitants were not rational, that one could not depend upon the application of reason and good behavior to achieve the greatest good for the greatest number, that—why not go whole hog? —life was very likely futile and meaningless, that Einstein's theory of relativity and Heisenberg's principle of uncertainty ruled the world, that it was no longer possible to hold off the realization of the death of the old mechanistic clockwork universe of the nineteenth century or the old world of Newtonian physics with its arrangement of harmonies and forces, of differential and integral calculus, and of the natural symmetries and orders that arise from checks and balances. Einstein and Heisenberg and Freud had finally broken through everything and come to describe the world of society, business, politics, and my own daily life.

I was discouraged by the world, and I was in favor of saying to hell with it. I was for dropping out and into my own private world. I was for instant gratification and to hell with the future—if there was to be any. Soon enough I was for smoking dope and popping pills and, if possible, the moment I got off the plane in San Francisco in 1967, I was for going directly in my rented red Mustang (rented red Mustangs seem to be a point of stability in my life) to an ongoing marathon orgy that would last the afternoon and into the evening and on through the next week with opportunities to get to know girls and boys, men and women, women and men and girls and boys in groups and singly together and apart—though mostly girls, because it was girls that the nuns had always forbade, never boys, and so girls I always thought about, smothering whatever normal homosexual urges I might have developed with thoughts of girls in every way along with a seasoning and spicing of fashionable vegetarians, nudists, mantra chanters, yogis, hermits, sadists, masochists, saints-manqué, crazed murderers, and macrobiotic freaks.

I walked down Haight Street in the late summer of 1967, past free stores that dispensed food and clothes and shoes and beads to all who needed them, free of charge, past the shops and galleries full of psychedelic art, the pulsating light shows, the circles of chaos within the well-ordered squares that were meant to recall Tibetan mandalas, past boutiques hung with Indian fabrics. Everyone was very friendly and welcoming then. Pot was being sold on the corners, or given away by the handful and by the rolled joint. Within a block and a half of my first arrival in the Haight, I was smoking a joint of marijuana that had been handed me on the street.

Girls carried bunches of purple lilacs and handed sprigs of the lilacs to young men as they passed them on the streets, and I fell in love with a young woman with curly red hair, Afro-style, a necklace of seashells, and tasseled belt, and then with a young woman in a leather miniskirt and Indian moccasins and leggings, her breasts covered with beaded bits of wampum, the whole costume topped off with jangling peace symbols of all sizes and colors and fashions made of metal and clay and ceramic.

And it was true that orgies were available everywhere—sort of true, in a way. At the end of Haight Street or at the end of Ashbury, whichever it may be —I have no idea to this day which street is which—I strolled into Golden Gate Park and there spotted the friend of a friend of mine from New York, named Kendra. I wanted immediately to go to bed with her. A stroll down Haight Street (or Ashbury) was enough to make anyone want to go immediately to bed, and the fact that she was the friend of a friend, or even if she had only been the friend of a friend of a friend, was in those days enough of an introduction to invite a young woman to go to bed. The vegetation in Golden Gate Park is unbelievably lush and verdant. To one accustomed to the foliage in the Northeast, it seems to be tropical or at least semitropical. It is big vegetation, full vegetation, juicy vegetation, luxuriant vegetation, erotic vegetation, and the denizens of Haight-Ashbury were spilled down the side of the hill, lying and lolling about, embracing and napping and smoking pot and gazing into foliage and listening to the musical group that had set itself up at the bottom of the little hill as though in an amphitheater.

Kendra was wearing a black sweater. She was a brunette with small fine gold rings in her pierced ears, many rings on her fingers, and handmade dark brown leather sandals and brown eyes. She was happy to see me, as everyone in Haight-Ashbury seemed to be. That Kendra and I had a friend in common seemed somehow both magical and profoundly significant. Everyone, as the Hippies quickly discovered, had something in common. For some reason, this surprised them—perhaps because they found that they had something in common and had mutual acquaintances with people not at school or in the same hometown but in some far-off and alien city where they had never been before. These were youngsters who had never traveled and who discovered all together and simultaneously and as an entire generation that they all had things and friends in common. It was enough to make them think that everything is related to everything else and All is One. Kendra and I lay on the hill in the park, smoking her marijuana, listening to the music, and chatting about the theater group that she was involved with there in Haight-Ashbury and about her roommates and about New York and about her family and about her brothers and sisters. We, Kendra and I, were as brother and sister. Many of the others there on that hillside were as brothers and sisters to one another. We all were enjoying a prolonged childhood innocence.

She took me home with her at last, to a sparely furnished room, decorated with Indian silks and posters of rock stars, on the top floor of an old woodframe Victorian house where her friend Michelle, a younger girl, with long blonde hair and a long, full white dress lay stretched out, reading and dozing, among the pillows on the floor. Michelle must have been no more than fifteen or sixteen. She seemed to me very much a child. There I was—my fantasy of an orgy come true, with two beautiful young women— and I was suddenly overcome by conflicting feelings. I felt regret that Michelle was not home somewhere being taken care of by her parents, whoever they may have been. She was too young. She needed, if not her parents, then certainly not a lover, but rather, an uncle, and I hardly felt avuncular, lying on the floor smoking pot between two girls.

Soon, we were looking idly at Michelle's copy of the I Ching, and Kendra cast the sticks to read my fortune. As Kendra went on with this lengthy proce-dure, it was clear how it would all come out: I was destined to take part in a very affectionate and pas-sionate orgy with two young women; but the I Ching is tediously elaborate, and the business of reading it is interminable, and the whole procedure was, finally, awfully soporific. I fell asleep. At my orgy in the late 1960s with two beautiful young women amid mari-juana and incense, I fell asleep.

So there I was in Haight-Ashbury, opening up to life in all its forms, experiencing the intense pleasures of pot and casual sex, giving play to the full range of my emotions, living for the moment free of constraint, winging out to enjoy the forbidden joys of life—asleep, in my dreams.

I was enraged at myself for the lack of purpose. I had gone through a full twenty-four hours in Haight-Ashbury without engaging in an orgy, without even making love with a nice, properly introduced middle-class young lady majoring in art history.

Nonetheless, I was watching these people very closely, and I was taking it in, sorting it out, storing it up for later use. In fact, the denizens of Haight-Ashbury were doing for me just what groups and individuals are supposed to do for their fellows in a free society: They were experimenting for me. They were trying things out—taking in peyote and coke and horse and speed and banana peels. They were testing these things for me. They were my laboratory. I watched as they foraged on the frontier and tried out my fantasies. Pot: OK. Acid: dangerous. Love affairs: a pleasure. Banana peels: a joke.

They were a congenial lot, these kids, middle-class whites most of them—and they were not as much in rebellion as they liked to think. Most of them, I suspect, had listened to their parents tell them for a dozen years that the materialistic life of suburban homes, cars, gray flannel suits, lonely crowds, treadmills to oblivion, and martinis were not everything, that there was some vague something more to life. The children listened well, and went out to look, to do what was expected of them, to live out the fantasies their parents could only dimly dream of.

Some of these youngsters burned themselves out with their fantasies, some frazzled their brains with acid, some are permanent wrecks. We used them—or I did. After a while, not right away, but after a while, after I had seen what went down, what worked, what I could absorb in my life, what I could not, I picked and chose among the things they tried for me.

It was not thought proper in certain circles in the sixties to check into a hotel in a strange town. One flopped, or crashed, at the pad of a friend or stranger. I moved into the apartment of a friend of another friend of mine in an old white Victorian house several blocks away from the center of the Haight-Ashbury scene. On the door of this house, in red paint, was inscribed the injunction: DO WHAT THOU WILT. On the first floor lived Bobby Beausoleil, leader of the rock group The Magic Powerhouse of Oz, a keenly slender fellow who sported high leather boots, leather pants, a broad leather belt, a blue turtleneck sweater, a necklace made of turquoise and what seemed to be bones, and a black top hat. Several years later, he would surface again as a member of the Charles Manson group.

The apartment in which I flopped belonged to a young filmmaker and photographer named Roger, who inspected my fat little plastic bag of marijuana and informed me that I did not know the first thing about how to clean marijuana properly. So before we did anything else, we sat cross-legged on the floor in front of the fireplace, which Roger had decorated with an assemblage of Oriental bells and incense burners and doodads and other thingamajigs, and cleaned my marijuana, removing all of the last little bits of seed and twig from the stuff, in an operation that was as clean as anything that has ever occurred at Massachusetts General Hospital and as solemn as anything that has ever been performed in a Greek Orthodox church. Having cleaned the stuff, we consumed some of it and proceeded to decamp to explore and partake of life.

We got in the red Mustang and drove several blocks to pick up Roger's friend Susan, who was a voluptuous young woman in a tight, tense body. She was nervous and frightened, but she had large warm eyes and ample lips and lovely small breasts, and it seemed she wished to feel more at ease and enjoy herself, as I did. She was interested in Roger and not in me, but we liked each other, and we both relaxed, and it felt good to be in the same car with her. We went from her house to the A&P where we pulled up at the curb and all got out and went in to pick up some supplies from the herb and spice counter. We got some ground allspice, some celery seed, curry powder, cumin seed, cardamon, dill weed, fenugreek, chervil, coriander leaf, basil, marjoram, arrowroot, cream of tartar, paprika, mace, mint, sage, pepper, nutmeg, rosemary, and thyme, among other things. We were going to sniff it and smoke it.

Roger had heard that cinnamon was a wonderful thing to smoke and so we had gone to the A&P originally to pick up some cinnamon, but people were smoking everything in those days. The great favorite was bananas, which required an extraordinarily elaborate preparation. We had no time for bananas. Roger wanted to pick up a package of Wheaties, but Susan and I talked him out of it.

The powdery stuff was for sniffing—the arrowroot,

cream of tartar, paprika, mace. The rest of the stuff
was for smoking. Marjoram and basil and coriander
leaf don't have much of a kick to them but they are
good as "vehicles." That is to say, what you really
want to smoke is stuff like curry powder and cardamon
and fenugreek and cinnamon, but you can't just roll
a lot of cinnamon into a cigarette paper. You need to
have the cinnamon carried by something the cigarette
paper will comfortably hold. And so you sprinkle dried
parsley into cigarette paper and then sprinkle a lot
of cinnamon on top of that and roll that up, and it
makes a wonderful smoke. We all shared a joint of
marijuana first as we were heading out on the Golden
Gate Bridge, just to give us a head start, and then we
started in on the other stuff, sniffing and smoking, and
it is a fine thing to be high on the Golden Gate
Bridge on a brisk crisp morning and a fine thing to be
high driving into Marin County through the rich
suburbs where the housewives go to the supermarket
wearing their clean white tennis dresses and looking
slightly crazed on affluence and pills and slightly sex-
starved and desperate for love. So it seems, at least, if
you're driving through the countryside smoking rosemary and thyme and sniffing black pepper.

Somewhere on a country road in the midst of Marin
County on a lovely hillside full of rolling fields of grass
and trees, I pulled over to the side of the road unable to
see well enough any longer to drive, sneezing and weep-
ing and laughing. I was beginning to feel as though I
were having some sort of asthmatic attack. I had in-

haled half of the A&P spice rack and on the whole, I think I would rather have been smoking Wheaties.

We got out of the car then and walked out into the fields and rolled in the tall grass in the sunlight and in under the shade of the trees and looked up through the leaves and into the sky, as children do.

I was going flat out in Marin County on only the tamest of vehicles. The old outer world was coming apart like a blasted pomegranate, shattering and de-materializing, and I was zinging into the old Heisen-bergian universe, in a way that I thought for a fleeting moment my cousin Charlie would have been proud to see. The reality of the outer world dropped away, and I saw, in that brief time, a miniature model of the whole of the decade of the sixties, of my sixties at least: As the outer world came apart, I came apart with it, sliding into a controlled breaking down and putting back together of my nerves and psyche that skittered on through the whole of the sixties and some-what beyond. What finally happened to me in that decade of rampage and fracas is that my subconscious, so long feared and held in darkness, so long repressed, so long kept in check for fear of the havoc it would wreak, was opened up. More than opened up, my sub-conscious broke through into my everyday and daily life and began to accompany me wherever I went.

I ceased to believe that I, or anyone else, was alto-gether rational, and I commenced, a bit at a time, to try to live with some parts of myself that I had formerly tried to pretend .(embarrassedly) were not mine: some large chunks of unlived adolescence of which illness had deprived me and that I now, awkwardly and, at that advanced age, childishly grasped at; some large chunks of sinfulness that my religion had denied me; some chunks of madness that the eighteenth-century Enlightenment and Harvard College had tried to drum out of me; some chunks of lust that my upbringing had tried to repress; I tried to reclaim all these and some other parts of my lost or unacknowledged self.

As I opened myself up, the first thing to come out was disappointment and rage, just as these surprising and frightening feelings came out of so many other young men and women, boys and girls. With Kennedy, I had learned to project my wishes out into the larger world. With the Vietnam War, I let loose much of my private anguish. I was enraged. I had been betrayed. I had been let down. Promises had been broken. I was not taken care of by my President, by the grown-ups, by my father. I raged against the war. I hated Johnson. I hated Presidents. I had come to believe that all the good guys, all the men I had been taught to respect as a child, were in reality the bad guys. They had led me into war, and I was among the wounded. I raged and burned; I plunged into fits and tantrums; I cried out against injustice; I savaged, self-righteously, those who disagreed with me; I shrieked and snarled and raved and every once in a while, upon occasion, from time to time, when I felt really mean, just to show that all along it was I who was the mature man of sweet reason, I would speak temperately against the war.

Then with Nixon the gorge rose again, and having practiced on the Vietnam War, I was ready for him, and my anger turned into a murderous fury, and I impeached him; I impeached him and, with him, I impeached all fathers, I charged all fathers with high crimes and misdemeanors; I impeached Nixon; I impeached all Presidents; I impeached my father, and most of all I impeached myself, the worst and phoniest father of them all; I impeached the uptightness, the shabbiness, the pretensions, the corruptness of myself; I impeached the Boy Scout facade I hid behind; I impeached my childish self and my adolescent self and laid bare the adult so that I could impeach him, too. Impeachment had become a habit, and I had become filled with self-hatred and contempt. I hated what I had grown to become. I hated my transparent pose of calm self-assurance; I hated the way I covered up the terrified, hate-filled, grudge-driven, self-pitying, bitter adolescent in me; I hated my naïveté and my timidity; I hated the boy-father, the father-manqué in me, and I hated, finally, my own rage and self-hatred. I wished to take myself apart and put myself together again, and so I impeached myself and exiled myself, removing myself from friends, family, and all the world, committing multiple ax murders and suicide all at the same time.

These were violent passions, without any doubt, and yet I cannot even now quite bring myself to apologize for venting such feelings against the Vietnam War or against Richard Nixon. I am sure I shall never find any worthier targets for hatred, and I have the feeling that the knack of politics consists not so much in denying these irrepressible private urges when we come to judge the public world but rather in making certain that we check out our well-rehearsed private feelings to see that they are justified and to see that we know which ones to call upon and when to call them up. My regret now is not that I expressed such anger but that, being surprised by it and wondering at its force, I modulated it too strictly. I wish I had given it fuller vent; I wish I had summoned up all my reserves of rage; I wish I had called up a lifetime of it. And then I wish I had been purged of it all. I thought, perhaps, I could vent the last of it on H. R. Haldeman. I hoped that when I met him it would be easy to hate him.

When at last, that Saturday in Los Angeles, at one o'clock, Haldeman pulled up in a blue Thunderbird, wearing a green blazer, green and yellow striped tie, gray slacks, brown loafers, and a genial smile that showed a radiantly clean and somewhat too regular set of teeth, shiny, well-scrubbed, tanned face, large, friendly eyes, he was terrifically anticlimactic, an appalling comedown from the passions and issues of the life and death of fathers and Republics. I was terribly disappointed. He looked quite healthy, solid, well-fed, relaxed, comfortable—and, worst of all, he appeared perfectly harmless and likeable. He hardly looked as though he had suffered from his ordeal. He seemed altogether untouched by it all. We drove through Beverly Hills.

HALDEMAN: How do you like Los Angeles?

MEE: It's a nice town.

HALDEMAN: Some people really don't like it.

MEE: Really? No, I think it's a nice town. Interesting shades of green.

HALDEMAN: What?

MEE: The different shades of green are interesting; they seem strange to me, coming from the East. We don't have these yellowish greens.

HALDEMAN: Oh.

MEE: In the plants, the foliage.

HALDEMAN: Oh, the plants!

MEE: Yeah.

HALDEMAN: Oh, yeah, the plants.

MEE: Is it green all year round?

HALDEMAN: Yeah, pretty much all year round.

We went to the Polo Lounge of the Beverly Hills Hotel. I ordered iced tea, and Haldeman brightened. What a good idea! He'd have one too. Iced tea was just the thing for a warm summer's day. He drank a lot of iced tea, pitchers of it, always kept some in the refrigerator. Did I like iced tea? Did I drink it often? So he was nervous. Phony and nervous and smiling. So was I. I had, fleetingly, a shameful, a disgusting thought that I am embarrassed to mention: I hoped he liked me.

I asked him what sort of book he had in mind.

He was thinking, he said, of a book that would cover the whole Nixon administration, with a chapter on Watergate, but only a chapter, and go into the organization of the White House staff, the decision-making process, the appointment-making process, the foreign policy process, the Vietnam process, alluding along the way to organizational structures, staff functions, and their structures, and . . . uh . . . functions . . .

I felt my brain begin to fall loose around my ears, and I began to slip, drifting sideward into inattention. I heard a man talking, and the words poured out, syntactically correct, even impeccable. I could have stepped to the blackboard and diagrammed each sentence as it blanded out onto the table. Here come the paragraphs:

Paragraph 1, subcategory A, subcategories 1, 2, 3, and a, b, c. Neat. Like talking to a grammar textbook, or a man who had suffered brain damage from a stroke. People who have suffered certain kinds of strokes often lose all ability to use words that mean anything; their speech has no content, but it is always grammatically perfect. My mind wandered.

After lunch, after the iced tea, we went to the shiny men's room in the Beverly Hills Hotel, stood side by side at the urinals, and, for some reason, at that moment, a question occurred to Haldeman, the first time that he had any curiosity about me: "Do you have any children?" Yes, I said, I have a thirteen-year-old daughter and a seven-year-old son, wonderful children, whom I missed while I was out in California. No other questions occurred to Haldeman.

We drove through Beverly Hills and into Hancock Park, a neighborhood of surpassingly prosperous middle- and upper-middle-income suburban American living. Haldeman explained to me that his house was nothing very special, that it was quite a modest home.

It was, in fact, a snug and pretty little imitation Tudor house with a well-clipped lawn. Haldeman and I went directly up to his study on the second floor. He made me feel immediately at ease, gesturing me to take the comfortable TV chair. He was in a relaxed and agreeable mood, and I asked him about his collection of books. He replied that most of his library was still in boxes, but that these were a few of his books about the Presidency and particularly about the Nixon administration. He had read, he guessed, most of the books that had been written about Nixon, and had annotated a good many of them as well. To illustrate this, he took one of the books off the shelves and riffled through the pages to show me how he had marked them. He had used three different colors of Magic Markers in underlining passages in these books. Green Magic Marker indicated that the passage was favorable to Nixon and Haldeman. Yellow Magic Marker meant that the passage was worth noting, though Haldeman made no judgment on its accuracy or value. Red Magic Marker meant that the passage was wrong. Haldeman had copied the passages marked with red ink and had set these passages out on pieces of eight-and-one-half by eleven-inch paper with his own rebuttals to the charges made. He showed me some of the sheets on which he had argued with the authors of some of the Nixon books, and I was stunned—not

merely by Haldeman's orderliness, which was formidable, not only by Haldeman's thoroughness, which was
painful, but also his ability to persist, his interest in
spending the hours and the days in copying out all of
these passages and replying even to the smallest point,
whether a criticism of Nixon's attire or Haldeman's
haircut, in exhaustive and exhausting detail.

Haldeman went to his file cabinets then and took
out one manila folder after another and handed each
one to me for my examination. Folder after folder after
folder came out of the cabinet, notes on books, drafts
he had made of chapters for a book he would write,
or a book he would have someone ghostwrite for
him. I took as many of Haldeman's files as I could fit
into the large canvas bag that I had brought along
for the purpose, and Haldeman took me back and
dropped me off at the Beverly Wilshire Hotel. I took
my canvas bag through the lobby furtively, the way I
would carry parts of an atomic bomb through the
lobby of the Beverly Wilshire Hotel. I went straight up
to room 832, making certain that I was on guard at all
times against potential muggers and document thieves.
In the room I slipped the bolt and threw the chain
and then placed the bag carefully, just so, next to the
glass-topped desk. I cleared the desk of its impediments,
of papers, books, stationery, tape recorder, tape cas-
settes, and then I sat down at the desk and commenced
to take the folders out of my bag, one at a time, carefully, reverently, knowing that I was handling historical
documents. I laid each folder in the center of the glass-

topped desk and opened each one ritually, as though inspecting some ancient parchment. They were all, all of them, every last one of them, absolutely empty.

Perhaps I exaggerate somewhat. The Haldeman files did in truth have papers in them on which words and sentences and even whole paragraphs had been very neatly typed, and so it may be uncharitable of me to say that these folders were empty. However, in all of these pages, in all of these folders, there was nothing about the eighteen-and-one-half-minute gap on the tape recording in the Oval Office, nothing about the secret plans to bomb Cambodia, nothing about the inner council discussions about the Phoenix program in Vietnam—in short, nothing that anyone who wanted to know what really went on in the Nixon administration or in America, now or in the past, at any level high or low, would want to know. There was a good bit of gossip and chitchat in the files about choosing a dog for Nixon, about movies that the President watched, about the swimming pool at Camp David and other folderol and balderdash and—how shall I say?—detritus, but there was nothing in these files that told of the way the Republic had worked in our recent past. Haldeman was trying, as almost all political figures have almost always tried, to beguile me with the false revelation and the counterfeit exposé, with this gossip about dogs and movies, to enchant me so that I wouldn't notice he is saying nothing about Vietnam and Watergate. I was amazed.

I put all the folders neatly back into my canvas

bag, making sure to keep them in the proper order, just so, neat, and clean, and well-ordered. I did not mention to Haldeman my disappointment with his top secret files. What the hell? I told him they were interesting. Were they not? In a way? And I met with him for several days, four or five or six days, after that, sometimes for the whole day, from nine or ten o'clock in the morning until five or six in the evening. We filled one tape cassette after another, I don't remember how many, and we numbered each one of them very neatly, very precisely: 1, 2, 3, 4, 5, 6, 7, . . .

We talked in his study and in his den, we talked on his patio and sitting by his pool in reclining chairs with our eyes closed, we talked in the shade and in the sunshine, and as nearly as I could tell, at that time, and later on, reading over the transcripts that were made from our tapes, he said nothing. It was, I think, a feat, a remarkable feat, one I have never seen duplicated, one that I would rank with any circus act, any feat of derring-do, any performance on the high wire. He said nothing; he never tripped, never hesitated, never fell, and always smiled.

I got nothing out of him, and I guess it was my fault. I had not pressed him enough with questions. I had not gone in for the kill. But others had tried that, well-briefed attorneys had tried that and failed. In truth, he stopped me cold for some reason. I found I could do nothing for a time but sleep too much, and think to no good purpose. He had slipped away from me. He had been reasonable and pleasant and bland,

and I could get no grip on him—or I felt, when I tried, as though I were somehow unreasonable, unpleasant, and deranged.

The problem was, first of all, that the old malefactor wouldn't say anything. He really was one of the great flat-out bores of our times, and I was heartily disappointed that my erstwhile monster was not worthy of my pervasive fear. He turned out instead, in his agreeableness and evasiveness and easy cordiality, to recall Hannah Arendt's observations on the banality of evil.

The problem was, too, that I identified with him still. I wished still that I had had his job, that I had had his power, that I was capable of doing what he had done without feeling remorse. I wished I could have his house and his car and his money and his suntan and his sense that all was right with the world and that he deserved the privileges he had and that the less fortunate had no just lien on his power or money—and all this without remorse. I envied him. I envied his assurance in the world, his appearance of health and normality, his upper-class WASP assumption of rectitude and good cheer that makes all who complain seem maladjusted, flawed, in need of a change of attitude or class. I envied him—and so I could hardly condemn him.

And the problem was also that I suffered still from an excess of unspent rage, and his boring geniality offered no good target for that rage. I suffered from the depression that predictably followed the spending of anger in which I had indulged, the act of regicide in which I had participated. And, of course, among other things, I felt discouraged and frustrated to think that Haldeman and Nixon were not in jail, to think of the apparent futility of all good effort, to see that Haldeman was tanned and fit and fine and to feel that, finally, there was no justice in the world. And so I was angry, with no good way left to vent my anger. I consoled myself then with the thought that Haldeman had to be burdened with a dread of the past, with what he still had to smooth over. He must smile, it occurred to me, and he must not hesitate, for others had hesitated, and they had gone to jail. He was not a free man, Haldeman; he was the captive, still, of his own reign of terror. Politics is indeed the act of self-creation, and Haldeman had turned himself into the citizen of a police state. It was a small consolation, but it was a consolation.

Then, at last, his blandness and his evasiveness and his anxious cordiality, combined with other bits and pieces of our encounter, brought me to realize finally that it was Haldeman, and not I, who was afraid; it was Haldeman, and not I, who had to live in anguish and in fear of the truth of his own life and history. And with that he began to die for me, and my spirits started to revive. My encounter with him had turned out to be a tonic, and the rage that I had been gathering over the years and unloosed on Vietnam and Nixon, and the aftertaste of that rage began to fade. I began to get my bearings again. I began to awaken again to the understanding that one moment of my history need not bind me as it had Haldeman, that I was not condemned to live my life in one decade or one period of my life, accepting a part for the whole, but rather that I could accept the experience of my whole life and history, grateful for the life that has been given me, knowing that I can rely on it, admitting that I treasure it, thankful for the knowledge that I can survive bad times, relishing the way that my past encourages me to go on freely, losing my confidence and finding it again, enjoying the adventure of it, delighting in making up my life as I go along.

I don't imagine that my own change of mood immediately transforms the reality of the outer world. I don't imagine now that my country has suddenly become a vision of democratic utopia. Not at all. But, having gone through the Nixon purgative, and having lived through a brief reprise with Haldeman, I feel I can give up my anger now and go on more equably. They had forced me, those two, to reconsider my past and to gather, at last, the courage of my own convictions, to remember that my urge for liberty must be linked with the urge for the greatest freedom for all, and that that in turn, in order to exist, demands justice and decency for all. It finally occurs to me that this is not a matter for anguish and rage. It is a matter to be pursued with pleasure and high spirits suited to the fineness of the task. Freedom is itself the most wonderful of things, and its pursuit is the most generous act possible.

I do still fuse my private and public worlds. The urge is irrepressible. All visions of the world are autobiographies. We all project our own needs, fears, fantasies, even psychoses on the public world. The humble thing to do would be to admit our distorted, personal, view of things and cease pretending we can comment rationally on the world, on politics. But even such objective fellows as my physicist cousin Charlie have stopped declaring that their mathematical formulas describe a "real" world, that they can know objective truth, or even that truth lies in the material world. They talk now, instead, in terms of "models" and only models, saying that their formulas no longer describe anything but a model of the world, that we may have no hope of truly knowing the world itself anymore, that all we know is the model that we know, that what we know is what exists in the mind, that what we know is a mental construct. Reality approaches solipsism. The universe, said Alfred North Whitehead, "is a giant thought."

It would be modest of us to go away quietly in the face of this knot. And yet, what is to create our shared world any longer now—now that the old objective Newtonian universe of checks and balances has been shattered, now that our old rational Enlightenment institutions have broken down, now that we live in a world more clearly described by Heisenberg and Freud and Whitehead—what is to create our world now if not precisely our openly expressed thoughts, our fears and wishes?

And how shall we make our shared world habitable for us all if we do not have the expression of our private fantasies modify and accommodate those of others? If we do not all enter and live in the public world in this way, then we shall have allowed the fantasies of only a few shape our world, and in that way, we know, lies a kind of national madness.

Lying on the grass in Marin County, smoking chervil and fenugreek, I formulated my conclusion, as nearly as I can remember, thus: We shall need a new understanding of democracy, its necessity and its rationale—a holistic view, an integrated understanding, of ourselves and of politics, that encompasses both the unique individual and the body politic, that is less formalistic and less Newtonian, and that is, at the same time (ideally), self-regenerative, dynamic, and heuristic. (Of the heuristic part we can be certain; heuristic is assuredly a word from the sixties.)

We drove on in the quick red Mustang, Roger, Susan, and I, on into Marin County, on north of San Francisco, near Fountain Grove, California, where, in 1875, the Brotherhood of the New Life was founded by the mystic and poet, Thomas Lake Harris. We were at Morning Star, a Hippie commune out among redwoods and apple trees. We left our Mustang in a large clearing at the bottom of a hill, and we set out on foot up the path—a narrow dirt path where one had to walk single file, Indian fashion. As we hiked up into the woods, we encountered young men and women—all of them naked—living in huge hollowed-out trees, or in tents and lean-tos that they had pitched, or in rude log cabins, or, on occasion, in splendid soaring tree houses. One of these tree houses was a beautiful structure as light and buoyant, it seemed, as a twig, as strong as the tree trunk itself, as enclosed and as open to the breezes as the leaves overhead. A young couple was making love in this tree house and as we approached they paused a moment and looked down over the edge and smiled at us.

We kept hearing music filtering through the trees, music of all sorts—music coming from flutes, from recorders, from all sorts of little nymphlike woodwind instruments; music coming from guitars, and, to top it off, the sound of human voices chanting the obligatory Hare Krishna, Hare Krishna, Krishna Krishna, Hare Hare, Hare Rama, Hare Rama, Rama Rama, Hare Hare. We lit a few joints and followed the sound of the Hare Krishna off a side path and more deeply into the woods.

We emerged at last, after several hours of exploring, and of greeting the youngsters in the woods, at the main house of Morning Star, the gathering place for all the Hippies who lived scattered on the mountain, the place they came to see one another, to pick up their mail, to sing and dance, and to have their communal meals. The house was a simple old mountain shack with several large rooms and a porch overlooking the gorgeous valley. We emerged from the woods as the residents of Morning Star were beginning to form into line in front of this house for their meal.

They had brought with them their tin plates and cups and spoons and forks. They were a happy, laughing, casual lot, in no hurry for their meal, enjoying one another's company, content to sit about on the ground and sing or tell stories or meditate. Roger, Susan, and I wandered into the house and into the kitchen where there was a vast iron pot on an old gas stove.

The kitchen was a shambles of boxes and cans discarded on the floor and open barrels of flour and sesame seeds, open cans of sesame oil with layers of dirt on top of them. The cook was smiling and filthy. Everyone was smiling and filthy. One had to pick one's way carefully across the kitchen floor to avoid boxes and cans and slick spots; and the packages, with their chewed edges, showed the evidence of active mice. The pot itself held a bubbling mass of God-knows what-all kinds of chunks and bits and blobs and smears of stuff. The flies flew around the pot and inside of it, and were cooked right in with the rest of the meal.

In the living room of this house and on the porch overlooking the valley were youngsters who were passed out and huddling against the wall, covered with old army blankets, with faces looking feverish and pale, the young men with dirty matted beards, over which flies and other insects crawled.

Would we like to stay for lunch?

Roger and Susan hesitated, and I was overcome by the old nightmare in which one runs and runs and gets nowhere. For some reason I could not speak. I think perhaps I was afraid that if I were to speak I would shout out: "What? Stay for lunch in this shit-house?"

I could not fathom why Roger and Susan hesitated. Perhaps they were seized with some other similar malady. I finally managed to mumble something about the need to get back to San Francisco. Roger and Susan pretended that they really wanted to stay, and I mumbled and muttered some more, and they began to smile and grin and shuffle their feet and back out of the door of the house with me.

We could not simply walk out the door and vanish, however. We had to walk back past the long line of those waiting for their meal, and the walk was an ordeal. As we walked down the line, each of those waiting with their plate and fork and spoon and cup would say, "Can't you stay? Won't you stay? Please stay and eat with us. Wouldn't you like to stay the night?"

Have I called all these youngsters dirty? I should not have. Some of them were handsome or beautiful and clean and well-scrubbed and healthy and glowing, but not many. Not many. To each of them we had to explain: No, we had to leave. No, we had to get back to San Francisco. Thank you very much. No, it wouldn't be possible, not this time . . . perhaps another time. Perhaps we might come back. Thank you very much. No, not this time. No, it just wasn't possible. No.

Hands reached out to touch, to hold, to hug, to shake hands, to pat on the back. Fingers and hands and arms entwining and grasping and holding and embracing, but no, we kept saying . . . no, thank you very much. No, no, it just wasn't possible.

A young woman stepped out of line and held my shoulder and looked directly into my eyes. She was a beautiful girl of perhaps eighteen years of age, with long dark hair down her back and dark brown eyes, high cheekbones, widely spaced eyes, a lovely slim figure, with lovely slender hips and full breasts and, yes, warm deep dark brown eyes and she said to me, looking directly into my eyes, "I would like for you to stay. Wouldn't it be funny to sleep in a tree house?"

In her eyes, amid the brown, I saw little shards of exploding yellow, and, in those little shards of exploding yellow, I felt a kind of drug-blasted desperation that I knew I could not handle. It terrified me. I was completely panic-stricken. I might have said to her, "No, you come with me. Come back to San Francisco with me." And anything I would have done from then on would have been better than what I did do. I said no, I must go, and I turned and walked back down the path toward the car.

Roger and Susan followed me, and down the path as we walked by the untended field of corn and other vegetables on which the commune was unable to bring sufficient members together to work, to grow anything to eat, we passed by the other building at Morning Star. This, the second building, was a barrackslike structure, raised a few feet above the ground on stilts with one large room and perhaps a dozen bunk beds.

This was the black ghetto. It was populated entirely by a gang of vicious-looking blacks. These were not love children, nor were they smokers of hashish or marijuana. These were hard-liquor drunks and heroin addicts. They drank beer out of cans and one of them shot up as we were going by. They called out to us as we passed and asked for money, and several of them came lurching and reeling off the front steps of their shack to come down and panhandle us. They were much enamored of Susan and circled her, looking her over, and Roger and I coughed up tribute money. I make them sound more threatening than they were. They offered us no harm and seemed indeed to be cordial enough. As we left they bid us good-bye with good cheer, but then a couple of them turned on one another and engaged in a savage knife fight.

These youngsters were trying, as I was, to live in a world beyond politics. They, too, seemed to have been hurt, been disappointed—who has not been?—and they wished to transcend the compromises and corruptions of the life of the political animal. But they did not escape politics for long. The worst form of politics caught up with these prodigal sons and daughters. They had managed—it was quite a feat really—to transport their own personal little black slum, complete with alcoholism and switchblades, out to the unspoiled wilds of California and to create, blacks and whites together, with their racism, their hedonism, their lack of regard for the landscape, the future, their dirty children, or their intellects, a grotesque parody of the very worst of the world they had wished to escape.

One heard a lot, those days, about the death of Western civilization. Joseph Campbell, then a professor at Sarah Lawrence and always a great student of mythology, suggested to me one day that I ought to read Oswald Spengler's *Decline of the West*. Frank Manuel, a distinguished professor of intellectual history at New York University, gave me the same advice. Then one day I noticed that Henry Kissinger had given a copy of Spengler's book to Richard Nixon. Kissinger, it turned out, had written his senior thesis at Harvard on Spengler, Kant, and Toynbee.

Spengler published his book just after World War I. He proposed, first of all, an apparently novel way of looking at history; he proposed that we view history not as a straight line of progress that culminates in the fineness of our own age but rather as a series of cycles, of beginnings and endings, births and deaths. In fact, Spengler's idea was not altogether novel: Giovanni Battista Vico had proposed a similar notion in the eighteenth century. The sociologist Pitirim Sorokin was at work on a similar idea, as was the anthropologist Alfred Kroeber. But, never mind that. Spengler said that the West had come to the point, in its own cycle, of inevitable, helpless decline. As with the death of most cultures, the West was coming apart under a succession of awful wars, an exhaustion of ideals, a mere surrendering of liberties and a welcoming of the order produced by Caesars, with cities that

CHARLES L. MEE, JR.

have ceased to be centers of creativity and become drains on the vitality of the surrounding countryside, a faddishness that replaces genuine originality and inspiration in the arts and in ideas, a "second religiousness" that celebrates mindless pseudo-religions without any deep understanding of real religious mysteries, a rootless, atheistic, and materialistic urban proletariat, brutish and ignorant of traditional values, rebellious and angry—in effect, a new "barbarian within."

For a while back there at Morning Star, Spengler seemed terrifically plausible. And yet his thesis will not stand. Spengler saw the whole history of the world as being divisible into Eight Cultures, and he built his theory around them. Not many years after Spengler's book appeared, Arnold Toynbee, working with the same basic vision of cycles of birth, life, and death, divided the history of the world up into thirty-one cultures instead of eight—and so happily perceived Western civilization as approaching a time of wonderful rebirth. Who's to say whether Spengler or Toynbee is right, or whether there have not been twelve cultures, or nineteen and a half?

Spengler's theory is riddled with built-in logic problems. Why, for instance, should we view cultures as organisms with predetermined times of birth, growth, decay, and death? Why not view cultures instead in the way that we view families, with many generations, sometimes dying out but sometimes self-renewing, with the possibility of survival through collateral branches? Indeed, why use such an analogy at

218

all when one can confront history directly and see its ebbs and flows, some short historical spans and some apparently ever-renewing? Why speak of the inevitability of cyclical movements when, if history demonstrates anything, it demonstrates an enormous capacity for complete surprise?

Spengler and Kissinger might well have agreed that the Hippies were a symptom of an inevitable new Dark Age. Toynbee, toward the end of his life, still agreed with the observations of the Toynbee of the twenties. Asked what good the Hippies were in the nineteen sixties, Toynbee answered cheerily: "If you had asked a citizen of the Christian Roman Empire whether the Anchorites and Stylites were performing any valuable function by withdrawing from society, he would have replied that by withdrawing from it they were saving it."

As it turned out, neither Spengler, nor Kissinger, nor Toynbee was quite right. We were neither doomed nor redeemed by the sixties. And yet we were certainly changed. Toward the end of the decade Joseph Campbell said to me that we live as though in a great open field strewn with the ruins of many myths and many civilizations. It is as though we might look about the rubble field and see here the head of an ancient Greek statue, the arm of an ancient Roman statue, a bit of remains from Pharaonic Egypt; shards of Babylonian civilization, bits of crumbling fresco, of Tantric or Zen design; paintings from the monasteries high up in the Himalayan Mountains; bits of bronze sculpture from the Orient; old rusted iron weapons; gold bracelets and earrings. It is as though our civilization lay about us in bits and pieces, apparently disintegrated. It is for us, Campbell said, to find the patterns or to start afresh out of the rubble heap. What Campbell was describing was hardly a world in perfect order; yet, if he thought he was describing a Dark Age, he was certainly not describing an epoch that seemed gloomy to me. He was describing a time of greater and greater freedom and possibility; he was describing the most wonderful of times.

Not all of these thoughts occurred to me while I was with Beatrice. Not even I lay claim to such insane compulsive interior monologuing. But some of the thoughts occurred to me—and the rest of them were, in some sense, necessary before Beatrice and I could get together. It is a heavy conclusion, this: to imagine how much garbage I have gone through just to arrive at a point of being able—again—to be alive and fresh, confident and spontaneous.

Beatrice and I felt good to one another; and we kissed and hugged and tickled and stroked and licked and made love with one another, over and over, on the pillows that we pulled down onto the floor in the living room, on the old woven Indian rug, rolling over onto the polished wide boards of the floor, surprisingly accommodating and friendly as they were. We came to rest from time to time, nestling together under the soft Scotch blanket, our heads variously happy on pillows or on the floor or held in one another's hands.

Her eyes were at once direct and soft, steady and receptive, far different from those eyes at Morning Star, but brown, too, brown with flecks of yellow, minuscule shivers of green and olivine, eyes that looked both outward and inward at once.

We made love, freely and affectionately, exploring one another's bodies, though trying nothing very dazzling, making no attempts at technical virtuosity or inventiveness, engaging in none of the newly fashionable sadomasochistic pleasures, remaining, both of us, old-fashioned, romantic, thinking of old-fashioned words such as *soixante-neuf* when we came naturally to that, dozing and drifting and then, soon again, embracing again, our bodies swimming against one another, drifting and fading and rocking, dozing again together, waking and making love again, our bodies completely fused, neither of us knowing where our beings began and ended, coming together, holding, fading together, suffused and drifting in and out of sleep and small kisses and murmuring of love.

People don't make love the way they used to. I am not complaining about the fact—far from it—nor making a technical point either. Technique may change, to be sure; one does not imagine Benjamin Disraeli engaging in certain modern practices, but that is the least of it. Having lived with Freud and Heisenberg, with hallucinogens and women's liberation and rock and mantras and ragas, we think and feel differently; we sense and see differently; we dream differently; we reinvent—doubtless each generation does, sorting its way through different pasts, pains, and pleasures—we re-create trust and love.

After the end of the sixties, early into the seventies, I was in London on some business for *Horizon*. The business was as much an excuse as anything: I was on a pilgrimage to see Arnold Toynbee. I am not quite sure why I admired and loved the man as much as I did. I hardly knew him at all, and I disagreed with much of his understanding of history. Yet I agreed with him in some tangential fashion, with his spirit, however imperfectly I knew what it was, and I took him as my guru.

I met him at his offices in the Royal Institute of International Affairs in St. James's Square. He was an old man then, in his early eighties, just a few years short of death. He was frail, and all but entirely deaf; his hair was pure white, and his skin was almost transparent in the sunlight that came through the large windows opening onto St. James's Square. He was unfailingly polite and solicitous and warm. His handsome, three-piece chalk-striped suit fell loosely around his frame; he was shrinking to nothingness inside his clothes; he was dematerializing.

We sat in large leather armchairs and chatted quietly about this and that, sipping tea, our voices paper thin and lost, absorbed in the large room with its deep draperies and heavy woods, talking of his travels to sacred shrines in the Orient, of Borobudur and of monasteries high in the Himalayas.

It is usual, in such auspicious circumstances as

these, to ask the great man for his final word, his ultimate insight, his summation of the world, on what life and politics and history is all about, on what the past and the future and our struggles are. But, I did not ask. Instead, I barged ahead, declaiming the thoughts that were flinging themselves around in my head. I had Toynbee cornered; he could not escape; and so I talked on and on, seeking some confirmation from him.

I told him that I had become possessed by the idea —an idea that owed more, perhaps, to Kroeber than to Spengler or Toynbee or the others—that things flourish until they have realized their full potential, until they have reached their natural limits, or exhausted their possibilities—and then they die, or disintegrate and dematerialize or alter, or mutate, or change. A civilization that is basically materialistic, for instance, one that believes truth resides in material objects or the relationship and balance among atoms or particles, will explore the material world until it has run out of things to explore, until it has found its limits—or drifted, unknowingly, beyond them, until, for instance, physicists have so thoroughly explored the universe that they have discovered that they are now exploring their own capacity to generate new hypotheses, they are now exploring their own mental constructs about the universe, they are now exploring their own minds.

Toynbee was listening and smiling, and I was spinning my theories energetically. My voice rose from time to time in that vast, dark room on St. James's Square, rose to penetrate Toynbee's deafness, rose because of my own exhilaration, rose unconsciously so as not to be lost entirely in those old Victorian draperies, placed on the windows sometime during the glories of the British Empire. I told Toynbee (my unfailingly courteous captive host) that, at the point at which civilization has come up against—or burst or drifted through—its natural limits, at that point it dies, or is formed again around a new organizing myth, is reborn or is transmuted into a new life form, just as, today, we have reached the end of materialism. Our civilization, I informed Toynbee, is dematerializing; we are entering a new era, one in which we shall drift into the inscape of the mind, our last great frontier, and it will be even more exciting than the Renaissance. It is not a matter of mere fads or enthusiasms for Zen and sensitivity training and psychological jazz: All that is only the pop fallout of a truly profound exploration led by neurophysiologists and psychologists, structural linguists and anthropologists, into the structure of the mind. At the same time, and equally exciting—and far more frightening—our discoveries in genetics are leading us toward the moment, for the first time in the history of the species that we shall take evolution consciously into our own hands, shall create ourselves in an image we choose—or else decline to change as we choose. The prospect is truly Promethian. We shall, astonishingly and terrifyingly, first have an image, and from that image shall come new life. Mind will create matter; matter will express mind: life will be a creation of our imaginations.

Did it not seem, I asked Toynbee, that politics became an even more urgent matter in these fantastic circumstances? Would we not need an even more open, even more democratic form of politics and even much, much more freedom to make certain the future of the species remained open to all possible imaginings— rather than closing itself off and staking its very survival on the inevitably too-narrow vision of any one or any few? Did not the very needs of biology for an open gene pool require an open, democratic society? Was it not truer than ever that we create ourselves through politics, that politics determines who we are and, more portentously and wonderfully, who we shall become in body and spirit? Did he not think this was so? Did he not think I was right? Was this not so? What did he make of his own life and work? Toynbee seemed startled to have a question directed toward him at last.

"Yes?"

"What do you finally conclude?"

"Eh?"

"I say, what do you make of it?"

Toynbee smiled. He hadn't heard a word I'd said. He thought I was saying good-bye—or was he trying to get rid of me politely? No, I think he thought I was saying good-bye, and he was trying to be especially polite so as not to let me know how rude I had been for abruptly taking my leave. I was leaning forward in my chair, as though about to get up and go. He was surprised, but he did not seem to be offended. Toynbee rose from his chair, the perfect host, and extended his hand. He was a wonderful, warm old man.

"Oh, yes, yes," he said, quietly. "Yes. It's been a pleasure."